DEAREST FOLKS

DEAREST FOLKS

Sister Leatherneck's Letter Excerpts and WWII Experiences

Berneice A. Herron

iUniverse, Inc.
New York Lincoln Shanghai

DEAREST FOLKS
Sister Leatherneck's Letter Excerpts and WWII Experiences

Copyright © 2006 by Berneice A. Herron

All rights reserved. No part of this book may be used or reproduced by any means, graphic, electronic, or mechanical, including photocopying, recording, taping or by any information storage retrieval system without the written permission of the publisher except in the case of brief quotations embodied in critical articles and reviews.

iUniverse books may be ordered through booksellers or by contacting:

iUniverse
2021 Pine Lake Road, Suite 100
Lincoln, NE 68512
www.iuniverse.com
1-800-Authors (1-800-288-4677)

ISBN-13: 978-0-595-39325-1 (pbk)
ISBN-13: 978-0-595-83726-7 (cloth)
ISBN-13: 978-0-595-83721-2 (ebk)
ISBN-10: 0-595-39325-X (pbk)
ISBN-10: 0-595-83726-3 (cloth)
ISBN-10: 0-595-83721-2 (ebk)

Printed in the United States of America

To:

Joseph James and Mary Lillian (Carey) Herron

My "DEAREST FOLKS"

Contents

PROLOGUE ix

AUTHOR'S NOTE xi

OUR EARLY YEARS 1

RURAL SCHOOL TEACHING 5

OUR FIRST BIG TRIP—1939 9

AMERICA'S RESPONSE TO PEARL HARBOR 11

OUR TRIP TO CALIFORNIA—1943 15

OUR LONG BEACH FRIENDS 18

WORKING AT CALIFORNIA SHIPBUILDING
CORPORATION (CALSHIP) 20

ELEANOR RETURNS TO MINNESOTA AND
BERNEICE'S PROMOTION 25

BERNEICE EXPLORES THE SERVICES 28

WAITING FOR ACTIVE DUTY ORDERS 32

SOME FUN THINGS WE DID WHILE IN BOOT CAMP 37

AWAITING OUR FIRST ASSIGNMENT 40

EL TORO AND INSTRUCTIONS BEGIN 43

A TRAUMATIC EVENT 51

MOTHER'S ILLNESS 53

AN UNUSUAL EXPERIENCE 55

BIRTH OF THE UNITED NATIONS 57

REHABILITATION INTERVIEWERS AND
COLORADO SPRINGS 62
OUR TRIP TO CATALINA ISLAND 65
VJ DAY CELEBRATION and PATTON—DOOLITTLE PARADE 68
OUR SEPARATION PARTY 71
THE CALIFORNIANS 75
A NOTE TO ALL READERS 77
A DREAM 79
A MESSAGE FROM THE COMMANDANT 81
MY NINETIETH BIRTHDAY 82
EPILOGUE 87
PHOTOS FROM THE EARLY YEARS 91
TEACHING MATERIALS 99
EXCERPTS FROM LETTERS HOME 105
POEM 163
BIBLIOGRAPHY 165

PROLOGUE

This is a true story of two sisters, Eleanor M. Herron, and Berneice A. Herron, from a small farming area, in southwestern Minnesota. It tells about how they responded to their "Uncle Sam's Call" after the attack on Pearl Harbor, on December 7, 1941. It describes their early days, as Rural School Teachers, and their decision to go to California to work in Defense. You will read about their trip, their life in "Eagle's Nest", their employment in the largest and fastest shipbuilding corporation in the US, their exploration of all Branches of the Service, and their decision to join the "MARINES.'

During their two years, eight and a half months in the Marines, they taught Aircraft and Ship Recognition to Marine Fighter Pilots; after V.J. Day these were assigned to be Rehabilitation Interviewers and helped interview and discharge Women Marines, from the Corps.

Most of their tour of duty was spent at El Toro Marine Air Base, at Santa Ana, California. Being in California afforded them the opportunity to see most of the famous Movie Stars, dance to most of the Big Name Bands, to visit many of the ships that came into the L. A. Port, and to attend many interesting functions, including the one, and only, big, "*PATTON—DOOLITTLE PARADE*" in L. A.

During their days on Active Duty, they wrote home almost every single day. Their mother kept all their letters, in a suitcase. Now these letters are in plastic sleeves, in notebooks, and are almost like a diary of those busy, interesting, dynamic days spent in the Corps. Excerpts from many of these original letters are included in this book. After the demise of the author, these letters are to be given to the "*WOMEN IN MILITARY SERVICE FOR AMERICFA MEMORIAL FOUNDATION*", in Washington, D. C.

AUTHOR'S NOTE

I wish to acknowledge the assistance I have received, in writing this book, from my only niece, Janyce Maree (Brennan) Hanish, and my grand-nephew, Sean Brennan. Without their most valuable help, skills, and insistence, this book may never have come to fruition.

Both of them have been firm in their commitment to the publication of this work and without their constant, and firm resolve, I am afraid I would have given up on the project.

Sean ordered the computer, for me, and taught me the basic skills needed to type my story and to print it. He currently is one of the Academic Department Directors at the Art Institute of Tampa having formerly worked on Wall Street, in New York.

Sean received his Bachelor's Degree in Graphic Design, from the Ringling School of Art and Design, in Sarasota, Florida, and then two Master Degrees from the Pratt Institute, in New York City.

Both Janyce, and Sean, are very skilled in the use of the computer and have edited, and arranged "my stories" so they are ready for printing

Janyce helped place all the original letters, that were written home, in plastic sleeves, and it is she who named the book, "Dearest Folks".

OUR EARLY YEARS

My sister, Eleanor Margaret Herron, and I, Berneice Ann Herron, grew up on a 240 acre farm near the small village of Dundee, Minnesota, near the Iowa and South Dakota borders, in southwestern Minnesota. Our parents, Mary Lillian and Joseph James Herron, had purchased and moved to this farm in l910. They moved there from Iowa, where they had been married in 1904 and where their first three children were born. Our oldest sister, Mary Celestia was born mentally challenged. Alice Mercedes was about two and Joseph Donald was a baby, when they moved to Minnesota. Eleanor and I were both born on that farm.

We had happy childhoods and very loving, optimistic, kind, and generous parents. They were deeply religious but never wore their religion on their sleeves, but exemplified their religion in their actions and in their response to relatives, neighbors, and friends. This was best demonstrated by the way they lived. Their home always had room for "one more."

In their very early marriage, Dad's nephew lived with them until he was married; a brother of Dad's, who was ill, lived, and died in their home. Shortly after Celestia was born our maternal grandmother, Mary Ann Carey, came to live with them to help care for Celestia who needed considerable care. Later on two more paternal uncles. a maternal aunt, and a cousin spent several years as members of our immediate family, five of whom were buried from our home..

The last person to live in our family was an old farm hand who had become almost like a relative. He had worked for our family when Eleanor was a baby. In his last years he developed Alzheimer's, was cared for by my parents, and died in our home.

When the first three children were born our Dad affectionately called Celestia "Biggie", Mercedes, "Middlety", and our brother, "Littlety." It was ironic that "Biggie" remained like a little girl, and "Littlety" grew to over six feet in height.

Our home always seemed to be a gathering place for relatives, and friends. Part of this may be attributed to the fact that both Mother and Grandma Carey were excellent cooks and bakers and our home was always filled with music. In 1894 Dad made himself a violin which he played, very well, for many years. He never took a music lesson so played "by ear." Mother never had any music lessons either but could accompany him, on the piano, by playing chords. Later on Doc played chords and sometimes accompanied Dad.

Berneice could play any song that she heard, "by ear", and both Eleanor and Mercedes took some music lessons. Later on Eleanor, and I, had friends, who were brothers, and who played in their family's dance orchestra. My friend played the concertina, and Eleanor's played the violin. They contributed a great deal to all the music that emanated from our home.

We all loved to dance and attended many house parties as well as other dances. We girls were all considered very good dancers, and felt a night was "completely ruined" if we missed one dance, which we seldom did.

Dad participated in some "Old Fiddler's Contests" and many times would win either first, or second prize. He would often just close his eyes and really "saw off the tunes." Either Donald, or I would accompany him on the piano.

We had many wonderful years growing up on that farm. We all had our "chores" to do, gather the eggs, bring in the cows, for milking, help set the table, help with doing the dishes, and other things commensurate with our age, and ability.

We had many carefree, fun-filled hours. Eleanor, and I, who later loved to travel, took our first trips vicariously, lying on a grassy slope, just outside our house, traveling "with the clouds." Eleanor would choose one cloud, and I another. We would then watch to see whose cloud went faster, and farther. Little did we know then that we would have the opportunity, and privilege, to travel, extensively, for well over fifty years.

We lived about two and a half miles outside our little village of Dundee. Very often our friends, from town, would walk out to our farm, where we would play ball, climb trees, look for bird's nests, wade in a creek that flowed through the back of our farm, play other type games, etc. Quite often in the winter we would meet our town friends half way, where there was quite a steep hill, in our neighbor's pasture. There we would all take turns sliding down the hill, in the snow, and across a small creek at the bottom of the hill. What friends—what fun.

It seemed that nearly every Sunday, as we were growing up, that we had company. This meant more cousins, or friends, with whom to play. As we grew older it meant more music, singing, dancing, etc.

Every night, as we grew up, Mother would gather all of us into the kitchen, for our night prayers. We would all be on our knees as she would lead us in saying the Rosary.

She also added a lot of extra prayers for many, and sundry people, and reasons. She also taught each of us, in turn, our Catechism. She loved her "Maker" and did her very best to instill that type love in each of us.

When Eleanor, and I, were about 6 and 8 years of age, we built a new house on the farm. Our old one had become too small and was torn down to make room for the new one. While the new one was being built, we had our kitchen in part of the garage, and we slept in part of the haymow. It may sound scary, but it was really quite a lark. It was in the summer and all the big doors in the barn, were open and it was nice, cool and exciting.

The story is told that when I was born, in March, our dog had just had puppies in under the granary. Our brother, Doc, would be about 5 years of age, and Eleanor two and a half at the time.. Naturally they were very fond of those puppies. Dad had warned them, especially Doc, not to go in under the granary to get out the puppies, as the granary could possibly give way, or the mother dog might bite them. However, the morning I was born, those two were dressed warmly and sent to play outside, as Grandma helped the Doctor with my delivery. Grandma then washed and dressed me and was sitting in a rocking chair when Doc and Eleanor came back into the house. Grandma invited Eleanor to come see her new baby sister. I must have made some whimpering sound that reminded Eleanor of one of the puppies. .Eleanor often said that she could remember circling the rocking chair a couple times and then began crying. Grandma asked her why she was crying and Eleanor is said to have replied, "That puppy has no tail." I have facetiously remarked, at times, "That was the beginning of a dog's life."

On quite a few Christmas Eve's, when it was impossible to get to town any other way, as the roads would be so blocked with snow,. our whole family, with the exception of Celestia, and either Mother, or Grandma, would bundle up, and set out, by foot, for our village, about 2 and a half miles away for a last minute foray into our Cooperative store, and then to Midnight Mass in St. Mary's church.

One special Christmas Eve, we had gone to Mass, and were on our way home about two or two thirty in the morning. It was a beautiful night, with a bright, full moon, but very. very cold. Right outside our little village was a rather steep hill that we would go down.

The snow was sparkling like diamonds, and it was more slippery than we thought.

One of our uncles, Uncle Dan, was living with us at that time. He was rather rotund and had his purchases in a sort of sack on his shoulder. I had happily witnessed him buying several different kinds of candy, when he was in the store, before church. He slipped on the ice, and fell with his sack of "goodies" preceding him down the hill. I must admit that I, at that time, never thought of his being injured, I was just worried that the candy might get lost.

When we arrived close to the house, we could see the reddish glow, out the windows, of the big hard coal stove that furnished the heat for the home. Inside it was toasty warm and a delicious dinner was on the table. The wonderful smells of all the good things cooking are still with me, today. Either Mother, or Grandma Carey, who was at home, taking care of Celestia, had prepared a complete duck, or goose, dinner, complete with all the trimmings. It would all be beautifully set in our dining room, and it would be ready for consumption by a cold, tired, but grateful and hungry family.

After that was all completed we all went to bed and slept rather late on Christmas morning. Early in the afternoon we would have our "tree" and then another delicious dinner on Christmas night. What beautiful and fun times we had.

These memories, and many others, too numerous to mention, are but a few we experienced in our early days on the farm.

RURAL SCHOOL TEACHING

Education always held a high priority in our family. Mother had gone to teacher's college in Early, Iowa, and had taught, in rural schools, in Iowa, for a time, before getting married in 1904.

After high school graduation, all three of us sisters, Mercedes, Eleanor and myself, attended one year of Teacher's training, at the Normal School, in our county seat of Windom, Minnesota, although in different years. Back in those years of the late 20's and early 30's, there were not many opportunities for girls to choose from. You could either be a nurse, a teacher, or you could do household work, for others. We all liked going to school, did well, and chose teaching as our profession.

There was only one Normal Training School, for teachers, in each county. You had to rate well in your high school subjects, in order to apply for admission to the Normal School. They only accepted 16 students, from the entire county, for any given year. We were all very grateful, and felt fortunate to be chosen to attend. Windom was about 25 miles away so we all did "light housekeeping" when we attended school, there. We would come home on the weekends.

I went to Normal Training during the school year 1932-33. When I graduated it was very difficult to obtain a position as there were many applicants for every school opening, and people with experience were given preference. I was only 17 years of age and I was looking for a teaching position.

Berneice's first year of teaching with her five Eighth grade graduates in June, 1934. Berneice (third from left) had just turned 18 in March, 1934.

It did not look too promising, but prayers move mountains. I was most fortunate to obtain a position in a nearly new school, which was considered a real "plum" and only about 8 miles from my home. It did have 32 students, all eight grades, and of course I had to do the janitorial work, as well.

I taught all subjects to all eight grades. For all of this I was paid the huge salary of $50 a month. After a very short time I began boarding out at one of the homes in the area and for my room, and board, I paid $14 a month. I would go home every Friday, after school, and return to my boarding place on Sunday evening.

I had a most excellent place to stay and I was treated like a family member. I still correspond with two of the daughters (one a first grade student and the other a 4th grader.) They both married, had big families and are now "grandmothers" many times over. That friendship has lasted these many years (1933-2006.)

I hope it never ends.

As a rural school teacher you had many "hats" to wear. You not only taught all subjects, to all eight grades, but you were doctor and nurse, if there was any accident, or injury; lawyer and judge if there was any dispute (and there were many); janitor (starting the fire, bringing in the coal from the coal shed, sweeping the floor, bringing in the drinking water from the pump out in the yard, etc. You also were expected to have a big Christmas program, including all your students, give each of them a nice present, prepare bags of candy, nuts and fruit, for each, and to prepare a big quantity of pop corn balls to be given to the younger, and older siblings of your students.

In the fall of one of my first years of teaching, I thought that I could stay home and "drive" to my school, about 8 miles away. My brother owned a Chevrolet couple, and that was what I was going to use. At that time you would have the road almost to yourself; traffic was almost an unknown. For a few days all went well; one night, however, I came out and tried to start the car. It would not make a sound. What was I to do? There was no one around for quite a distance. I tried, and tried to get it started.

Finally in desperation I lifted up the hood and looked in. I could just as well been looking into a deep well; I knew nothing about what I saw. However, I did know that there were some tools in a box, in the trunk I went back and got out a small hammer. With that I gently hit almost everything I could reach, got into the car; it started and purred like a Cadillac. So much for my mechanical ability. Shortly after that I started boarding out near my school.

During the first years of my teaching career, all three sisters were teaching in rural schools. Most of all our years in the profession, we had to board by our schools. We all were very fortunate as we all loved the people with whom we stayed and they were all very good to us.

One winter, however, I was "marooned" out at my boarding place for six weeks, due to severe blizzards and huge banks of snow. This proved no hardship, for me, however, as we had excellent food and I was young enough to enjoy playing the piano, singing, and playing all sorts of card games with the family .Their place was almost my second home.

We were living this very quiet life when our world was shattered by the news that the Japanese had bombed Pearl Harbor. This, indeed, was a tremendous shock. Our country was short of many vital necessities, one of which was rubber. During l942 it was amazing how the American people threw themselves into all kinds of drives and how many men thronged to recruiting stations all across this nation signing up to join all branches of the Service.

Every man, woman and child did what he/she possibly could to help in any and every "drive" I asked my students, ages 6-14, if they thought they could collect *used* license plates, so they could be recycled. Well, all anyone has to do is to motivate young children, and they will outdo themselves. Soon we had license plates up to our ears. I had told the students that I would give a prize to the one who brought in the most plates. One student "hit the jackpot."

His uncle had been collecting old plates, as a hobby, and he donated his collection. Naturally that little third grader won the prize.

That collection went so well that I then asked it they could collect "old tires." Again the students tore into action and the pile of old tires grew daily out in back of our school building. Rubber was a much needed commodity so we were very happy to do our small part. The school board members brought their horses and wagons, and loaded the tires and took them into town. Again a prize was given to the student who contributed the most to the pile of old tires.

OUR FIRST BIG TRIP—1939

In August of 1938, Eleanor, and I, were pleased that salaries were going a little higher, and the family really needed a car, so we, after a lot of planning, discussion, praying, and looking, finally purchased a new Chevrolet. How happy we were and how grateful we felt. We immediately named our new car," Blackie."

So, in the summer of 1939, we decided to take our parents on a nice trip. When we approached them about it, however, they declined. They were always willing to give their place to someone else and to wait for another time. We wanted to take them, but they insisted that we take some of our girl friends, and have a relaxing time after a hard year of work.

1939, All of us with our 1939 Chevrolet 'Blackie'. L to R: Kathryn Krogman, Eleanor Herron, Berneice Herron, Catherine Hullerman, Rosella Scully and Marilla Fury.

We invited four of our good friends to go with us and after much planning and discussion, six of us set out for what ended up being a 7,300 mile trip. None of us had been on any long trip before, had never seen a mountain, or an ocean. It is a good thing that we were all slender, then, as three of us had to sit in front, and three in back. We had no air conditioning, nor radio in the car, so the windows were rolled down and the hot air and noise, a constant companion.

We went through the Bad Lands, the Black Hills, Yellowstone National Park, Spokane, Seattle, San Francisco and the World's Fair (1939), then to Los Angeles, Hollywood, Long Beach, Salt Lake City. (where our car celebrated it's first birthday), Boulder Dam, Omaha, and home. We were gone for 7 weeks and we returned home safely with not a scratch on the car nor one flat tire.

While we were in Long Beach, California, we visited a girlhood friend of our mothers. Mayme Reuber and husband, Carl, had formerly lived in Iowa, but because of Carl's stroke, they had moved to California where they had purchased a fourplex, only two blocks up from the ocean. We had communicated with them and they were delighted to have us visit them. Little did any of us know that in such a short time we would all be in a war and that we would be seeing each other so soon, again.

AMERICA'S RESPONSE TO PEARL HARBOR

Most every American, who was living at the time of the attack on Pearl Harbor, can well remember when they heard President Roosevelt come on the radio, and make that unbelievable announcement!!! What a shock and what a real wake-up call It is so indelibly imprinted on our psyches, that most everyone can well remember what they were doing, and where they were at that precise moment.. Nothing, like this, had ever happened to us before. It was most difficult to even imagine.

Very shortly after this, more than one million Americans enlisted!!. The Selective Service Act of 1940, the first peacetime military draft in history, had put more than one million men in uniform and almost three million more would be drafted in 1942.

Three weeks after Pearl Harbor the government imposed rationing. First tires, then sugar, coffee, gasoline, meat, fats and oils, butter and shoes. Americans three themselves into all kinds of drives—rubber, tin, aluminum and scrap paper. All these things could be recycled.

Americans were very afraid after the attack and *ten million* volunteered for civil defense duty. German submarines soon were sighted off our East coast preying on our oil tankers and other merchant ships. Federal authorities began the incarceration of more than 120,000 Japanese-Americans. American and British strategists wondered how a *two-front* war could be fought, and won.

Since the Philippines and other far off Pacific possessions could not be held against an all out Japanese attack, the planner's decided that the Allies would only try to contain Japan's expansion in the war's early months and they would organize a massive strike against "Fortress Europe."

The Allies suffered some very humiliating defeats in 1942 before starting back on the road to recovery. One of the worst was the infamous Bataan Death March, in the Philippines and the Cabanatuan Prison, also located there.

Japan controlled almost 13 million square miles of Asia and the western Pacific. They, Germany and Italy had been planning this for 9-10 years, so the Japanese had all types of installations in the caves and tunnels of most of the islands they controlled. They had filled them with food, ammunition, and arms of all kinds.

President Roosevelt, however, rallied the American spirit by telling us that we were daily increasing our strength and soon we, and not our enemies would have the offensive

In top secrecy Lt. Col. James Doolittle and his fellow Army aviators were planning a very bold strike. On April 18, 1942 (on the 167th anniversary of Paul Revere's ride) they took off the deck of the aircraft carrier "Hornet" in the northern Pacific, and with Doolittle piloting the lead plane, sixteen B25's headed for Tokyo!

They dropped bombs on military and industrial targets in the capital, and five other cities, and then flew on the China. A storm and high tail winds is said to have helped them conserve fuel and helped to camouflage their planes. (Some of these brave men were taken prisoner after their planes ran out of gas and they had to bail out into enemy territory).

At about this same time another top secret work was under way in Hawaii. Navy cryptologists, bit by bit, were cracking the Japanese Naval code. They then told Pacific Commander Navy Chester Nimitz so our Carriers were deployed to the Coral Sea, northeast of Australia, where our first great naval battle was fought.

The Marines had also enlisted the assistance of about 400 Navajo Indians who had their own unbreakable voice code and who were of extremely great importance in transmitting battlefield messages. Their assistance to the Marines has been made into two movies: "The Code Talkers" and the "The Wind Talkers".

Most of the men were already in the Service, or Defense, and Uncle Sam really needed thousands, and thousands of employees for the shipyards and airplane factories. He truly needed *WOMEN* and they responded by the *THOUSANDS*.. *WE* were two of them.

In 1942, it is astounding how much was accomplished, with so little, in building up our defenses. We were just coming out of the Great Depression and our country had very little money to spend on building up airplane factories, shipbuilding corporations, and other type defenses. However it was almost miraculous how much was accomplished and how everyone cooperated, doing what they could in what needed to be done.

Our only brother, Joseph Donald, whom we all called, "Doc" was very patriotic and immediately volunteered for both the Navy and the Army. He was disqualified, however, because a few years prior to this, he had gotten his right hand caught in our corn picker. Although the Doctors were able to save his fingers, his hand was slightly crippled.

It never kept him from playing ball, hunting pheasants, or deer, etc. but the services would not accept him. He was highly disappointed. He did the next best thing, however. He, and some friends, went to California and found employment in a Kaiser shipyard, in Richmond, California, right outside San Francisco. There they worked on the famous "Liberty" ships, which were extremely vital after most of our fleet had been destroyed.

In February of 1942, the government embarked on a crash campaign of building these vessels and settled on this one design, which eventually was mass produced as swiftly as one every 80 hours. They were 441' long, 57' wide and could carry about 10,000 tons of cargo. The first one is said to have been launched 10 days after the keel was laid. About 2,770 Liberty ships were built with each one having a life expectancy of five years.

About 250,000 indispensable Merchant Marines and Seabees carried troops, munitions, food, and other supplies across the oceans and to the front lines of history's most far flung conflict. From Pearl Harbor to V.J. Day, 731 U. S. merchant ships were sunk, and 5,638 men died as a result of enemy action. The Seabees also constructed the much needed runways, bridges, roads, and other necessary buildings, etc., for all the armed forces and were more than willing to do whatever needed to be done.

By 1943 most of the men were gone into some branch of the Service, or were already working in Defense. Shipyards and airplane plants were desperately in need of hundreds, and hundreds more workers. Radios, newspapers, magazines and billboards all began begging and beseeching women to come work in

Defense. "Uncle Sam" began pointing his finger at you, and your patriotism was being severely tested.

Yes, we heard. Besides answering the "call to duty" the pay in these Defense positions was much better than we could make teaching school. Yes, we were patriotic.

So Eleanor and I decided that we would go to California, and work in Defense during our three summer months. She had already signed a contract to teach that coming fall. I had very recently broken up a very serious relationship, so I had not signed any contract. I felt that if I liked working, in Defense, I would stay in California, if not, I would sign a contract in the fall when I returned.

Eleanor was teaching in a school near Worthington, Minnesota, about 35 miles from home. She was so highly regarded, as a teacher, by her school board, and all the parents of her district, that they had offered her $150 @ month for the coming school year. This salary was the highest that had ever been paid in that county, up to that time.

Our dear Dad, Joseph James Herron, decided that he would go to California, to work in Defense, also. The family could well use the money he would make. I also think he was a little worried to have his two daughters go, alone, to California. He was an excellent sport, never complained about anything, helped do what he could to help us around our apartment, and worked hard at his position in the shipyard. We did realize that he missed being home.

OUR TRIP TO CALIFORNIA—1943

We were excited about going to California but we would be leaving our dear mother, and retarded sister, alone, at home. Our married sister, Mercedes, and husband, Vincent Brennan, lived on a farm about 15 miles from our little village, and they were very good to Mother, and Celestia, but we were sad about leaving them in our lonely little village. Mother, however, again assured us they would be O.K. but that we should write *often*.

This was the one "negative" about going to California; having to leave our beloved mother, and sister, as well as our married sister, Mercedes, husband and their children. However, Eleanor, and I, were determined that, if possible, we would find an apartment, in sunny California, and move our entire family, there. Minnesota's winter weather had really gotten to us.

Finally all preparations were complete and the day for beginning our "Tour with our Uncle" had finally arrived. We had communicated with our dear friends, in Long Beach, the Reuber's, and had been informed that there were "jobs galore", and that we could stay with them, for a few days, until we got settled, etc.

We drove our 1938 "Blackie" without air conditioning, or radio to Long Beach. California. What a memorable trip we had. We had very good luck—no accident, nor any flat tires. In several places, where we got gas, they didn't even ask for our "coupons", so that all helped.

From Kansas City we followed Route No. 50 almost straight west from there and went through Hutchinson, Kansas, where there were many oil wells, and salt mines. The largest salt mine in the world is said to be there. Then we went through Dodge City, KS after making 375 miles that day. We went through La Junta, Colo., where we stopped to visit relatives we hadn't seen, in years. We followed the "Santa Fe" trail and saw Pike's Peak, at a distance. We also read many interesting markers along the highway. Right outside of Trinidad, Colorado was a camp full of German and Italian prisoners. Further back, in Kansas, there was a huge Japanese internment camp. We also passed lots of huge air bases and saw planes of all kinds. We would stay at "cabins" for which we would pay around $3.50. We went over the "Raton Pass" and had very scenic sights. We went through Santa Fe and Albuquerque, New Mexico where we saw narrow streets, Spanish missions, Indian curio shops, and Indian Cliff dwellings.

Going through the desert was quite an experience. We drove through most of it during the late evening and early morning hours.. Even then the temperature was well over 100 degrees. When we stopped driving and got our "cabin" we were all exhausted and very thrilled to take refreshing showers and to get cooled off, as well as to get some much needed rest.

Finally we arrived at our destination—959 E. 2nd St., Long Beach, California, on a Saturday. Before going to their place, we drove down by the Ocean, so our dear Dad could see it, for the first time.

Berneice and Eleanor on their way to California, 1943

OUR LONG BEACH FRIENDS

Our trip made lasting impressions on all of us. We had never seen "concentration camp" signs, before; we had seen big, busy airports with many larger planes than we had ever seen and now when we arrived in California, we were very shocked to see all the "barrage balloons," and so many buildings, roads, bridges, etc. camouflaged . It really told you, in no uncertain times, that we were at war. We were also told that there were hundreds, and hundreds, of mines in the water right off the coast.

Mayme and Carl Reuber's home. "Eagle's Nest" was over their garage, 959 E. 2nd St. Long Beach, CA.

When we arrived at our friends home they had left a note, and a key, stating they were attending a funeral, but we should go in and make ourselves at home. They came home shortly afterwards. What a wonderful reception we had. They were just like family. We felt that not many people could go into a strange city and have a Welcoming "key"waiting for them. What friends.

When our friends, Carl and Mayme Reuber, lived in Iowa, they owned a car dealership. At one time they employed a mechanic by the name of Henry Eimers. Henry (Hank) had little, or no family, so as the years passed he became more and more like a son to them. He had been a soldier in WWI, and was very military minded. After Carl's stroke he helped both Carl and Mayme in any way possible and was a true family member.

We all visited, hard and fast. They lived in one of their apartments and the other three, as well as the small one, over their garage, were all rented. Apartments were very hard to come by as by now there were thousands, and thousands, who had responded to "the call" and were now also looking for apartments. It was said that some, who being denied access to an apartment, would actually "cry" as they needed one, so very much.

Again, prayers moved mountains, for us. The very first Sunday, we were there, the lady who was in the small apartment came to tell Mayme that she had been assigned a position, in Arizona, and would be leaving very shortly. What a break, for us.

Although it was really an apartment for one person, we gladly accepted it, moved in and very shortly thereafter we named it "Eagle's Nest." It had a nice sized combination living-dining room, small kitchen, one bedroom and one bath. Dad slept on a couch in the living room and we shared the bedroom. It was small but cozy, and it was "home."

Mayme Reuber, our great friend with Hank Eimer's Model A.

WORKING AT CALIFORNIA SHIPBUILDING CORPORATION (CALSHIP)

We truly "scoured" the papers looking at all the ads for employment. We soon decided that the three of us would go to a place called "Terminal Island" about l0 miles from Long Beach, and see what they had to offer. The big shipbuilding companies were located out there.

When we arrived it was quite a sight to see. It was a real eye-opening experience for two small town gals, that's for sure. There were numerous "time shacks" all around. In front of each one there were long lines of people waiting their turn to be interviewed. We went to the back of one line; finally Dad said he would go to another line that looked a little shorter, and then, hopefully, we would all finish about the same time. None of us knew it then, but he had gone over to a different shipbuilder's line.

After waiting for what seemed a very long time, we finally were up to the head of the line and had our interviews. They then gave us a typing test. When that was completed they told us that we qualified to be Senior Typists and we would be working for the California Shipbuilding Corporation—"Calship." They gave each of us a slip of paper that we were to present to a "policewoman" the following Monday morning, at Calship. Our pay was to be $.74 an hour, with time and a half for overtime. This seemed like "big money" to two former rural school teachers.

Dad had signed to work for the L.A. Shipyard and Dry Dock Corporation as a "tin fitter." He was to receive $.95 an hour.

The fateful day arrived!. Monday morning and we were to report for work at our new place of employment. It was about l0 miles out there. We had to walk about 7-8 blocks to catch the "Calship Special" which was really 5 streetcars hooked together, and it took us out to Terminal Island. Dad went to his job, via street car. He, too, worked on Terminal Island.

We were two of 175 new employees that Monday morning, waiting for the arrival of the "policewoman" and for the whistle to blow so the "graveyard shift" would leave the yard. When the whistle did blow, we were not prepared for the sight we were to see, or the noises we were to hear. Besides the whistle, music began blasting over the yard, and people of every shape, kind, size and description began pouring out the shipyard. They actually ran for the turnstiles where everyone had to have his/her lunchbox opened, and all men had to have their billfolds inspected, before they could leave.

There were all colors, all ages, all sizes, all conditions of people. It was a sight to behold. We later found out that Calship employed 43,000 people in its three shifts. No wonder there was such a number of people exiting the yard.

Coupled with all this commotion was the noise on the yard itself. With their many "ways" (places where they build a ship) plus the noise of the "chippers", the welders, and the looks of the huge "gantry cranes" with a full load of lumber beneath them, truly made an indelible impression that will never be erased.

The "policewoman" gave us a short talk, and then told us to follow her "closely" while she took us on the shipyard and to a big auditorium where we had a "safety film" and more instructions. She didn't have to tell us twice to follow her "closely." We were almost welded to her. After our film, and instructions, we were divided into groups, and then taken to our place of employment, according to the instructions written on the sheets we had been given at the hiring hall

Our building was a huge hip-roofed building which contained a couple offices, but it mostly contained all the material for the outfitting of the Liberty ships which were being built right outside our door. The material was stacked, row upon row, from floor to ceiling, containing all the various "bits and pieces" necessary for outfitting these ships.

It was a very large building so that trucks could come in and deliver, and load supplies. Workers would be in there to inventory all the material received. They would have long sheets of paper on which they would account for all material received. These accounts were called "MRR's. (Material received records.") After they had filled their long sheets, they would bring them into our department, where we had to type three copies of each, with nothing between the copies other than carbon paper.

When we were first introduced to our "supervisor", a lovely lady, from Chicago, she said we must be" from the Midwest." We wondered how she could tell. She said it was because people from that area always "dressed up" for their first day of work. We had on our Sunday best. We weren't going to let anybody know we were "country girls." Gladys Angstrom, our supervisor, was a wonderful person to work for, and with. She was kind, considerate, and inspiring. She worked hard, herself, and set a good example. She did have a physical problem, however, and would not be able to work too long.

Besides the 4-5 typists, and Gladys, we had 8 Auditors in our department. We were also part of a huge office. After we typists would finish an MRR, Gladys would have to go over and proof read it, to see we had not mixed up any numbers, etc. as all the bills, for all these interior parts of the ship, were paid by the top (white) copy that one of the typists had typed. After Gladys would proof them they would all go to the Auditors and they would go over them all, again. The auditors would then separate the MRR's, and the very next morning, the white copies would have to be "hand carried" over to the Pay office, from where the bills would all be paid.

It was extremely important that our MRR's were well done, or thousands of dollars could have been wasted. The number of MRR's completed in one day also indicated the amount of work that had been accomplished in the department, for that particular day. We had to keep "on our toes" and type as quickly and as accurately, as possible. It was a workout, but challenging, and important.

Soon after we began working there, Gladys confided to us that she would have to be resigning in early Fall and she would like to recommend one of us to take her place. This was rather "heady" news as we had not worked there very long, but it would mean a big improvement in pay as she was getting $1.05 and hour. Imagine that, at this time in our lives. Eleanor told her that she would be returning to Minnesota, so I would be the one to accept, but I did not expect to have it offered as I was so new on the job.

Eleanor, 1943

Dad, Berneice and Clare

L to R: Dad, Berneice, Mayme, Clare Carey (cousin) and Hank

ELEANOR RETURNS TO MINNESOTA AND BERNEICE'S PROMOTION

The summer passed very quickly. We loved our little "Eagle's Nest", we were having great fun with many interesting dates, much dancing, many movies, and we loved Long Beach. Soon, however, it was time for Eleanor to return to her teaching position, in Minnesota. Dad, and I, planned to stay at our Defense positions and to continue living in "Eagle's Nest." Eleanor truly hated to leave as she enjoyed her work, etc. and it would be the very first time in our lives that we would be parted. I, too, was very sad that she had to leave.

Our cousin, Clare Carey, and two other teachers, from the Midwest area, planned to ride home, with Eleanor. We were happy she would have company and they would help a little with the expenses. Eleanor was very loyal, her word was her bond, so she left for home. As most of them were teachers they were able to get enough gas coupons, for their journey Dad, and I missed her, very much, but we tried to "carry on." Dad was a "super" helper and I was so happy he stayed with me.

Soon after Eleanor left, Gladys resigned, and I was very *flattered* to be offered the position. What a wonderful "vote of confidence" and what a raise in pay. I was thrilled, but this was tempered by the fact that I now had a lot of responsibility, and pressure, to see that we completed many MRR's daily. Coupled with this I also needed to add a typist. This may not seem like a problem but typewriters were at a premium as they had all been donated to the war effort. To find a typewriter was like looking for a "needle in a haystack."

I was sent a lovely lady, much older than most of us, probably in her early 60's. It was quite evident she had not typed much in the last many years. The only typewriter that was available was one with a very long carriage on it. No one would have been able to accomplish much with it. So, she tried to do her best, but her MRR's were slow in coming, and messy when they did arrive. This slowed down the whole office procedure, so within a day, or two, I was informed, by the big office boss, that I had to "fire" her. I told my boss that I couldn't do that; he informed me that I *HAD* to do that.

That night I prayed and prayed as to what to say to her. The next morning I took her into a room and we talked. I told her that I was sure she was doing her level best, but she had a very poor typewriter to work with and that there were many other, perhaps easier jobs, in the shipyard that she might want to look into. She agreed and said that this was too stressful for her, also. We parted graciously and friendly. I *was most thankful* that it worked out so well. Her replacement was a "super" typist and helped us really get out a lot of "MRR's" daily.

Calship had a practice of allowing a certain number of its workers to have a little extra time, at noon, to observe one of the almost daily launchings of a Liberty ship. The day that I was given this privilege, we launched the "USS Carole Lombard." She was married to Clark Gable and had become the first causality of WWII. She was on a big Bond drive and was returning to California, when her plane crashed near Las Vegas and she was killed.

CLARK GABLE was there, that day, as well as his good friend, *JAMES STEWART*. They both looked positively "dashing" in their respective uniforms. Carole's best woman friend, *IRENE* DUNNE, broke the bottle of champagne over the bow. It was a real fun experience to see three great movie stars on that *one* day.

We had learned that the California Shipbuilding Corporation was considered the biggest, and fastest shipyard in the U. S, if not the world, at that time.

When I left this office to join the Marines, the entire office staff gave a "farewell party" for both Eleanor and me. They had delicious refreshments; all signed a "darling card" and they gave us a very nice suitcase as a going away gift. Quite a few of them corresponded with us while we were in the Corps and we were entertained by some of them when we returned to California, as Marines. They were all wonderful friends and made our days working in Defense very memorable.

Calship Farewell Party, February, 1944

BERNEICE EXPLORES THE SERVICES

In the shipyard we worked 6 days a week, so each week we had a different day off. About this same time I began to notice girls in the various uniforms of our services!! A light began to glow in me and I began to wonder why I was working where I was, and if there was something more *patriotic* that I could and should do! With my sister, my "better half" gone home, I was rather timid about approaching new things, but I did decide that I would explore the various services.

The only one I really knew, at that time, was the "WAC"s. On my first day off, I looked in the telephone directory to find the address of their recruiting office. I can still feel the mixture of emotions as I entered that office.

A very lovely recruiter greeted me, answered my questions and gave me several brochures so I could send some home to Eleanor. The fire was beginning to be ignited that WE would go into some branch of the service!!. Eleanor and I corresponded very frequently—this was the first time in our lives that we had ever been apart. It was not easy as we always had been extremely close. Our parents often could not tell which one of us was talking, or which one had written something. We were two and a half years different in age, but closer than many twins. We thought alike, spoke alike and wrote alike. We got along extremely well and loved each other very much.

At this same time, back in Minnesota, Eleanor was teaching in her rural school and receiving the highest salary that any rural teacher had ever been given, but she was missing the excitement of California, and was already yearning to return. Teachers were very scarce and *good* teachers almost impossible to find so she was very badly torn between wanting to come back to California and feeling it her duty to stay at the helm.

By this time I had now gone to see about the "Waves"—the Navy. Again I was welcomed with open arms, had my questions answered and received the brochures. The fire was burning brighter. My letters to Eleanor were beginning to ask her to resign from her position, come back to California as *WE* were joining the service!! By now *HER* fire was burning, too!!

When she spoke to her three man school board about her wish to return to California they began playing on her patriotism—which was more patriotic to do, join the Service, or stay and teach as she was such an outstanding teacher? They would come to her school several times a week and beg her to stay. She notified the County Superintendent, early on, that he should be looking for a replacement for her as she was returning to California as soon as a replacement could be found.

It was a very emotional experience for Eleanor but at Thanksgiving time some teachers graduated at Mankato Teacher's College and one of them was hired to take her place. This girl was a beginning teacher and we were told that she argued with the students as her boyfriend was in the Army, and the students argued *for* the Marine Corps.

In our almost daily letters home we were always asking our dear mother to come for a visit to California. If anyone needed a vacation, it was she! She was home, in our small village, taking constant care of our oldest sister who was mentally challenged. Mother was a beautiful person, inside, and out. She would always want someone else to get the new dress or take the trip. She was happy to make do with what she had.

Now would be a perfect time for Mother to come to California, as Eleanor would be returning. Although it was kept a secret, Mother *did* come with Eleanor, much to our *delight,* and *surprise*! Our married sister Mercedes and husband, Vincent Brennan, took our older sister, Mary Celestia, to their home and cared for her during Mother's weeklong visit to California.

Before this, I had explored the possibility of joining the Coast Guard, the "SPARS," and had found them to be *extremely* interesting. It didn't hurt at all that their recruiting gal was a stunning looking girl and she looked *"pretty as a picture"* in her uniform! They would train at Daytona Beach, Florida. We had never been to Florida at that time, so it sounded very glamorous and exciting. We were almost sold—UNTIL—

I began talking about my interest to join a Service, out in my office at the shipyards. One of the auditors said that I should look into the *MARINES*. I did not even know that they took women in that HE MAN outfit. He told me that the Marines had begun accepting women several months earlier. That was *news* to me but something that truly *excited* me, right from the start! I did not know ONE living Marine, at that time. I had only *heard* of them!!

On my very next day off from work, I found the Marine Recruiting Office and the rest is history!! I *CANNOT* begin to tell anyone my feelings of exhilaration, joy and excitement as I talked with THAT recruiter—a beautiful girl in a perfectly *SUPER* uniform. She gave me all the material I needed for both my sister and me. I left with a strong feeling, that God willing, both of us would soon be "*LADY MARINES*".

Mother truly enjoyed her week with us in the Eagles' Nest, although the weather was not nearly as nice as we wished it to be the week she was with us. We did have several of our friends in to meet her and we took in quite a few of the sights in the area including visiting the old Mission Capistrano.

Eleanor was so thin when she arrived back that we were afraid she would not pass the physical exam to join the Marines. She did however, and all was finalized for us to be sworn in to that prestigious corps.

Dad and Mother left for home, on the train, on December 14th. We were lonesome to see them go. They would have loved to see us sworn into the Corps, but felt duty bound to get home to take care of Celestia.

Finally the momentous day came—December 15, 1943! What a *THRILL* that was and how EXCITING!! We were now MARINES!!

After we were sworn in we decided we should CELEBRATE by having a good luncheon in a very NICE place in L. A. Where did we decide to go? To *Clifton's Cafeteria!* That was the most *beautiful* place two small town girls had ever seen. It had palm trees inside, birds in cages, waterfalls, good food and lots of interesting places to sit and eat. They also had a PIPE ORGAN!! That was really something.

We each had a good-sized tray of delicious food and we found an interesting nook, close to the waterfall, to sit and enjoy our special luncheon. Lo and behold, we had no more than started eating when the pipe organ began to play, "White Christmas". That was the *VERY FIRST* time we had ever heard that song. With our parents on the train, having just been sworn into the Marines, not knowing what all lay ahead, not going to be back in Minnesota for a white Christmas, was too much for two *brand new* recruits to handle. We both began *crying* and we *cried* so hard that we almost ruined our tray of food. Every time since, when hearing that song, that particular scenario comes to mind.

I was elated to find an article in 1990 regarding the Clifton's Cafeteria, written by Jane and Michael Stern. It stated that in the 1920's and 1930's many cafeterias were enjoying their golden age and had been built on the same epic scale and with the same architectural panache as the great downtown movie palaces. The article stated that one of the most spectacular and best remembered of the cafeterias was Clifton's Pacific Seas Cafeteria in L.A. It was opened in 1931 during the depths of the depression.

It was a success and not only because meals were cheap and diners could dawdle but also because they provided cheap entertainment in the form of dazzling décor. Patrons dined amidst waterfalls and tropical plants, artificial lava rocks and dramatic colored lights.

The original Pacific Seas cafeteria closed in 1960, but there are still other Clifton's going strong in L. A. They are happy to provide customers with printed copies of some of its best-known and most requested recipes, including millionaire pie, spinach soufflé gelatin, and the single most-requested recipe of all, Clifton's coleslaw. This simple, unimprovable formula goes back to the first cafeteria in the 30's and the Clifton family estimates that they have sold more than 20 million servings of it since the beginning.

I was delighted to read this article and to know they might still be functioning. That cafeteria made an indelible impression on two newly inducted Marine recruits in 1943. It will always be a treasured memory.

WAITING FOR ACTIVE DUTY ORDERS

Then came the anxious weeks of waiting for our Active Duty Orders. When Eleanor returned to California she was very thin. She wanted to get some type work for the short time before we would be going to active duty but we decided that she should get more rest and gain back some more strength, so she decided to keep up "Eagle's Nest", which she did in great fashion. That also made it very wonderful for me as she did all the laundry, shopping, cooking, etc. I would come home from work and have a good dinner all ready to eat. Then I could rest a while and then we would go dancing down on "the Pike". This was the beachfront where several dance halls were located and only about two blocks from our apartment. Many of the big-name bands played there, at that time, and there would always be hundreds and hundreds of service men in attendance. We had no scarcity of dancing partners. We both loved to dance and were considered good dancers at that time in our lives. We surely had oceans and oceans of good, clean fun and made many nice friends among our service personnel.

Every day when I would return from work the first thing I would check would be whether or not our active duty orders had come! We were getting very anxious to begin our new way of life. We had to be patient. We did receive many very interesting and beautiful Christmas cards during this time, and they were all specialized about joining the Marines.

Christmas came and went; it was a very beautiful and very special Christmas as it was our first one without a "white" Christmas and also our first one with no family present. Our friends were most generous, kind and loving, but it was "different." It made us realize that we were now on a different course and many new experiences lay ahead.

Finally one day is early February our Active Duty Orders *DID ARRIVE!* What an exciting experience! We would be boarding a troop train, out of L.A., on February 18th, 1944, headed for New River, No. Carolina. On February 18th, we went to L.A., had our evening meal at the station, and then boarded a troop train

Berneice A. Herron • 33

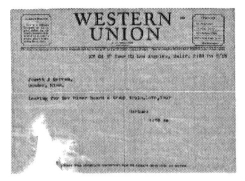

Leaving for Boot Camp, 1944. What an exciting day.

for our long ride across the USA. The Lady Marines had several coaches and the Men Marines had many more. There was no fraternization, whatsoever, all the way to Camp Lejeune, New River, North Carolina.

Eleanor and I were fortunate to be assigned to a compartment. It was very compact but we were happy to sleep in the bunks. Eleanor slept "topside" and I had the lower bunk.

Our food was good and during the long days of travel, we would play cards, sing, and do puzzles with the other girls. We all also did extra grooming, hair, nails, etc. We made nice, new friends but it was a long journey with little to do. We were allowed to get out of the cars a couple times to get a little exercise, but not for long. Every day we would ask the conductor where we were; so many times he would reply, "Texas", that we thought if we ever got out of Texas we would be at our destination.

After about 5 days we were told that we would soon be arriving at boot camp!! Little did we know what lay ahead! Buses met our train and took us the remaining way. As soon as we set foot off that bus, we were on a Marine Base, and we were spoken to in Navy lingo!

To most of us it could just as well have been Greek. Here we were to spend our next six weeks. It didn't take us too long however and soon we were talking that *LINGO* as well as anyone.

Well, here we were at boot camp, at Camp Lejeune, New River, North Carolina in the rainy spring of 1944. Soon we were assigned to our barracks and were beginning to live a different lifestyle. Again we were "bunkies" with Eleanor again on the top bunk and I on the bottom one. Our possessions included our bunks and a foot locker at the foot of our bunks.

We had many instructions before coming to boot camp about rules and regulations, length of our hair, what necessities to buy, and we were told that we would only wear our civilian clothes for a short time until we could be fitted for our uniforms.

Our Barracks at Camp Lejeune.

We were very precise about buying the proper things and were determined to be "good marines" in every sense of the word.

Among our instructions we were told that our hair could "touch, but not cover our collar." In order to be, according to regulations, and before leaving Long Beach, I determined to have a "cold wave". These had just come onto the market and were considered "the thing" as far as permanents were concerned. They were very expensive for that time, but I thought nothing was too good for going into the Marines. I remember I paid $45 for it and I was very happy and proud of the result. I thought I was all fixed up when I arrived at Boot Camp. $45, then, would be like $145 now!!

You can imagine my chagrin, when one of the first nights we were there, if not the very first, our Captain came into our barracks after dinner and had us all stand "at attention" at the foot of our bunks. She came around pulling each girls hair down to see if it was of the proper length. When she came to me, she pulled down my curls and told me to have my hair cut and to report to her office at 9o'clock the next morning!! What a shock and what a scare!!

I, who wanted to be a model Marine and here I thought I was in trouble already. I immediately asked her if there was a beauty parlor on the base. She replied that there was but no private would see it for 6 weeks!! What to do? The only scissors we had with us was a curved bladed manicure scissors! Eleanor was totally chagrined and we were both afraid that we were off to a bad start in our chosen Corps. Eleanor had me sit on the "foot locker" at the end of our bunk and she cut off my expensive cold wave as best she could. She must have done a good job as it passed inspection the next morning. I can tell you now, that that was the worst experience I had in the entire two years and 8 1/2 mo. I was in the Corps. I look back on it now and I think it was funny, but I certainly thought it anything but funny, at that time.

Boot Camp was a most challenging, interesting, dynamic experience. It was very "rugged" for that time. Men Marines were very reticent to take "skirt Marines" into such a He-Man outfit. However the Marines were experiencing such terrific losses in places like Tarawa, Saipan, Iwo Jima, etc. that there was no other choice, so they reluctantly gave in. They stated, however, that if women *did* come into the Corps. they could expect *NO* privileges, because they were women. The Marines also said that the women could not have any other name than Women Marines. We, therefore, have the distinction of being the *only* Women to have the same name as the Men in our Branch of Service. We have NO other name!

During our 6 weeks in boot camp we marched everywhere we went. We had various and sundry experiences. We had many classes about Marine Corps history and many other things. We marched through many muddy puddles, and were then opened up, for inspection, and told to be sure to shine our shoes. Some of our GI Instructors had recently returned from active duty in the Southwest Pacific and were not too enamored to have to be "Drill Instructors" to women. They would find some of the worst puddles, and march us right through them, and then scold us for dirty shoes.

We spent time in the Mess Hall, serving the other girls. We had Guard Duty, crawled along the ground as ammunition was being fired over our heads, climbed on ropes, climbed through barrels, etc. One day we had to put on gas masks and run through a room that was filled with noxious gas.

Everywhere we marched, marched and marched. We sang, often while we marched. We practiced for "Battalion Review." We learned and often sang the Official March of the Women Marines which is as follows:

Marines! We are the women members of a fighting Corps

Marines! The name is known from burning sand to ice-bound shore.

Marines! We serve that men may fight in air, on land, and sea;

Marines! The eagle, globe, and anchor carry on to make men free!

How proud we were, and still are, to sing this beautiful anthem!!

In the Corps we were also given tests of all kinds: personality, intelligence, aptitude, etc. We were being evaluated, also as to attitude, personality, aptitude, intelligence, etc. almost daily, but at that time we did not realize it.

It was in the Corps that our long and lasting nicknames of "Irish" and "Mick" were begun. One of Eleanor's Marine friends told her she looked so "Irish" that he was going to call her that. It was a good nickname, for her. She exemplified much of what is good about her nationality: good looks, deeply religious, friendly, humorous and kind.

One of my male friends told me I looked like a real Irish "Mick".. I did not know whether that was a compliment, or not, but it has lasted these many years. We were often called: "Irish and Mick of the Recognition Department." We always liked our nicknames, very much.

In earlier years we had been called "L", "Niece", "Bee", and for several years, we called *each other* "Seglo". I cannot, for the life of me, remember where that came from, or what it meant, but it was quite meaningful, to us, for quite a few years.

SOME FUN THINGS WE DID WHILE IN BOOT CAMP

One day while in boot camp, we were told that some of us would be able to go that evening to see an exhibition of the Marine "Devil Dogs." These were out at the edge of our base, quite a distance from any of the barracks.

These dogs were highly trained to be very ferocious. They had special handlers who loved those dogs and who worked with them and trained them. The dogs were several different breeds with many German Shepherds.

When we went out to see them we were told to stand in a certain place and not to make any sudden movement. You can well imagine we stood very quiet and very still!! The handlers put on a demonstration for us and we were all very deeply impressed by what the dogs were capable of performing. It was a very interesting evening.

One day the photographers from the *Look Magazine* came onto our base and wanted to take some pictures of the various activities of the Women Marines. Some gals were chosen to do a certain thing, and others did other things. I was one of those chosen to have a ride in the Higgins's Boat, out in the Atlantic Ocean. This boat was built by a Mr. Higgins, in New Orleans, and became very important in transporting Marines, and others, from their big ship onto the mainland. It had the ability to go in as close to shore, as possible, and then to drop a ramp for the military to exit on. It could then go back to sea quickly to get another load of military.

38 • *DEAREST FOLKS*

Berneice in Look Magazine—1944

This was the one and only time we got a ride in that type boat. It was interesting to us that *Look* photographers would take pictures of this as this was not something that Women Marines did regularly.

Of all the various pictures the photographers took that day, only a few were featured when the magazine came out. Ours was one of them. It was featured in the *Look Magazine* of June 13, 1944. At that time the magazine cost exactly one dime!!

AWAITING OUR FIRST ASSIGNMENT

After graduation from boot camp we anxiously waited for our first assignment. We did not care where they sent us or what we had to do, if only we could be kept together. This was shortly after the five Sullivan brothers, from Waterloo, Iowa, (Frank, George, Matt, Al and Joe) had been killed when the ship they were on, the USS Juneau, had been sunk off Guadalcanal. Shortly after that the Navy made a ruling that family members should be separated. This ruling was very much in our minds as we waited for our first assignment. We had asked all our friends to pray that we would be kept together and we really used the "hot line" ourselves. Prayers can move mountains and they certainly worked for us!

The day finally came and we were all assembled in a big room where our assignments were to be given. My name, starting with a "B" came before Eleanor's which started with an "E". When it got down to the "H"s we were holding our breath, as were our friends. Soon we were hearing, "Herron, Private, Berneice"—Cherry Point, No. Carolina, (everything was very silent), then, "Herron, Private, Eleanor"—Cherry Point, No. Carolina. There was a collective sigh of relief! We were so relieved and thankful to God for granting us our desire. We felt we could do anything the Marines required of us if only we could be kept together! We knew we had made it over the first hurdle.

Cherry Point, No. Carolina was a beautiful base, also. After more testing and evaluation, we were both assigned to "Aerial Gunnery School". We had many different kinds of classes, aircraft and ship recognition, link trainer, a little about rockets and also we had to learn how to take apart and put back together 50 caliber machine guns! The first day we walked into the room where this was taught, and we saw long rectangular tables on which these 50 caliber guns were mounted. This was almost too much. We were both deadly afraid of any type gun and wondered if we could ever do that.

We were told that in the Marines you could think what you wanted, but you didn't dare say anything. Under my breath I said to Eleanor, "My word, what have we gotten ourselves into now?" There was no response. We also had to learn the nomenclature of all the parts of the machine gun. We did not know it then, but later, as we taught our Marine Fighter Pilots, they flew their Corsairs with 3 of these machine guns in each of their wings. We had to know a little bit about the guns. We tackled the task of learning them and I am happy to report we succeeded. Don't ask me anything about them now, however.

Things were going well for about three weeks when, on a Saturday, our training school caught fire and burned to the ground. There went all our records. There were several fatalities, but there would have been many more had the school burned on a weekday when many more classes would have been in session .Now what would happen to us?

We were soon informed that we would be given a temporary assignment, on the base, while we waited word from Washington, as to what our next assignment would be. We were then assigned to help in the publication of the next Base Directory. This proved to be interesting and took quite a little while.

After this was published, we were assigned to be on "night duty" in the Women's Barracks, each in a separate Barracks. This meant that we would be in charge of that particular barracks all night long, and would be manning the front desk. The door, by that desk, was the only one open all night and all girls, had to check in, and out, at that desk. We also had to check, every two hours, to see that all the doors were properly locked, and that there was no fire in the building. The nights could have been very long, and lonely, but we would call the other Marines, both male and female, who had the same type duty in other barracks, and we would visit with them by the hour. That made the nights pass swiftly, and we had many good laughs. It really turned out to be a lot of fun.

Finally word came from Washington about our new assignments! What would they be and would we be separated? We had always wished that we could be sent back to California, as we really loved it there, but we thought that was too much to ask for. Imagine our surprise, and delight, when out of all of us there were to be assigned, five were to be sent to the big Marine Air Station at El Toro, California, not far out of Santa Ana, and we were two of the five!! We were thrilled, thankful, and simply delighted! We were to be assigned at El Toro, in the Ground Training Department, as Aircraft and Ship Recognition Instructors to Marine Fighter Pilots. To this very day I cannot but *WONDER* how we were given such an interesting, demanding, and responsible position in the Corps!

On several weekends while at Cherry Point, we had gone on some interesting and fun excursions to Raleigh, North Carolina, Washington, DC etc. One funny thing happened while we were going to see the Washington monument, in Washington. We had on our dress whites with our gold buttons and gold emblem. We were walking in step and feeling pretty sharp when we met a *WAC* private, who saluted us. Of course we had to return the salute so that she could never say she had met some Marine Officers who had not returned her salute. We had a good laugh as here were three privates saluting each other in the shadow of the Washington Monument. (She must have thought we were officers or she would not have saluted us.)

En route from the East coast to El Toro we had our first furlough home! How thrilling and wonderful that was. No matter how long one is in service, the first furlough home is always the one that is indelibly imprinted on one's memory. To be able to show your parents and family, as well as your friends, your new uniform is a great moment of pride and an unforgettable experience. What a great time we had. Soon it was time to leave for El Toro. Although we were sad about leaving our parents and family, we were thrilled to be returning to California and only a few miles out of our beloved Long Beach.

Nearly all transportation, for troops, was by train. Most all passengers on any train, at that time, were Military. One never lacked for friends to meet and converse with, on any train trip. It was great fun to share experiences and to learn from each other.

EL TORO AND INSTRUCTIONS BEGIN

Now we were Marines and back in our beloved southern California. How excited and thankful we were!

When we entered the gate at El Toro Marine Air Base, we felt we were in our second home, and how true that proved to be. Everything on the base was very new. Our base was constructed late in 1942 from an original bean field. Although many people might have thought it looked quite barren, we thought it was very beautiful. This proves that "Beauty is in the eyes of the beholder," for sure.

El Toro was basically divided into two main areas, one for the Fighter Pilots and one for the Torpedo Bombers (TBM's). Most of our work was with the Fighter Pilots but later on we were asked to teach Recognition "on the other side of the field". These Officers and enlisted men, of an entire squadron, would soon be out on carriers in the southwest Pacific. Prior to our going over to that side to teach, they had always been taught their recognition by their Intelligence Officer. We were happy and flattered when we were asked to go over there, as substitutes, and then be given the assignment to be their recognition teachers.

Now our real challenge was about to begin!!! After arriving at El Toro, we were told to report to the Ground Training Building and to begin observing in the classes that were being presented. Besides learning to recognize all the Japanese planes, the American planes, and the few British planes that were operating over there, the pilots also had to learn how to recognize all the Japanese ships, American ships and eventually, after most of the Japanese ships had been destroyed, the Japanese Merchant Shipping Tonnage, and submarines!!

After the Allies had sunk most of the Japanese ships, the Japanese resorted to Merchant ships to carry their troops, ammunition, food, supplies, etc., much like we had done at the beginning of the war, and for most of the duration.

In the Ground Training Building there were many different kinds of classes that the pilots had to take—navigation communications, First Aid, survival training, map reading, ordinance and gunnery and many more. Out in the flight area they had to become proficient in flight training tactics, night flying, rocket firing, bombing, field carrier landings, and many other things. They truly had full, strenuous, and exacting days. They were expected, by their Commanding Officers (CO's), to attend one hour of recognition each day. We taught the same syllabus each hour, for six hours per day, so the pilots could attend any hour that fit best with their other classes. We had to keep close records of their attendance as their CO's felt it was, or could be, a matter of life, or death, for the pilots to learn to recognize the planes that they would so soon be dealing with, out in the Pacific.

When we visited our first recognition classes as observers, they were being taught by our Recognition Officer, and a "super" Woman Marine, Ruth Goldstein from New York. They were working very hard but neither of them really wanted to teach.

Our Officer had other responsibilities and Ruth would much prefer to work next door in our office, maintaining the records, keeping up on the "Intelligence Reports", and being in charge of all the other duties that needed to be performed. They were both happy to have some new Marines that wanted, and loved to teach. Ruth, Eleanor, and I became very close (friends, and still are to this very day .We all loved our Lieutenant.

Ruth was informed that a young man, who lived not far from her in New York, was close by at an Army Base and she should contact him. She had never known him before. She did, and this led to a very serious relationship and eventual marriage. His name was Paul Horenstein. When she went back to New York to marry Paul, we sent her the following telegram, which she still has to this day.

"This day you have changed from the "Pot of Gold" to the "Horn of Plenty."

Paul and Ruth currently live in Scottsdale, Arizona. We visited them, at their home, and they have visited us, here in Sun City Center. Paul currently is not in good health.

We still communicate quite frequently. (I was just informed that our dear friend, Paul, passed away on March 2, 2006. He is buried in the Arizona Veteran's Cemetery. He was a wonderful husband, and a great father to their two girls.)

Our Lieutenant in charge of Recognition was very proud of "her girls" and did all she could to see we got our promotions, when available, and was very generous in signing for any, of us, to have passes whenever we could be spared to take a few days off. We especially liked to visit our brother, Doc, who was working in Richmond, California, near San Francisco.

We had sent him a telegram when we had been sworn in to the Marine Corps. His friends told us that he carried that telegram, in his billfold, and would show it, often. He was extremely proud and happy, that he had two sisters serving in the Military, although he had not been able to do so because of his injured hand. He came to visit us too, whenever he could.

When our training school had burned down, at Cherry Point, we had received about three weeks of training. The rest of our learning was up to us!! We *REALLY* had to study!!! We were determined to be good teachers and we realized that what we were teaching could well mean life, or death, to our pilots! We did *NOT* take our responsibility lightly!!! No one was going to stand up in front of a class of 50-60 Marine Fighter Pilots and give them any "bum steers." You would not have lasted, as their teacher, more than a minute. They were SHARP, in intelligence, as well as looks!!!

Their plane, "*THE CORSAIR*", was a real winner and you better know what you were talking about when you stood in front of the class, as teacher. We studied *CONSTANTLY* and our office received three types of messages and information from headquarters, in Washington—Restricted, Confidential and *SECRET*. Only Officers were supposed to see *Secret* material but after a time we were given permission to do so.

The Famous "Corsair".

It was not long before Eleanor and I were the only Recognition Instructors on base. What a *Challenge, Honor and Workout!* When one of us would be in the classroom presenting a lesson, the other would be in our next door office helping Ruthie, studying, preparing future lessons, and digesting the messages from Washington!! It was a *very* busy schedule and very demanding, but we *LOVED* doing it.

We taught mostly by slides that would project a very small image on a screen. In a matter of a tenth of a second the pilots had to discern whether the flash was a Japanese plane, an American plane, or a British one. They further had to tell whether it was a bomber, a fighter, or another type plane. (The British had but a few planes operating in the southwest Pacific) They also had to be able to distinguish ships, whether it was a Japanese, British or American ship and finally they had to study and be able to identify submarines and Japanese Merchant Shipping Tonnage.

We also had many models of ships, submarines, etc. to use in our classes. We fully realized that many of our pilots would leave our class, fly to San Francisco, then to Pearl Harbor where they would board their carrier and in a matter of 2 or 3 days they would be right out in combat.

Many times pilots who had been in combat, and returned to our base, would come in and thank us and tell us that what they had learned in our classes helped save their lives. What *SUPER* news!

The Japanese planes had such long and hard to pronounce names, that soon after the war started an army officer, Captain Frank T. McCoy, Jr., devised a system by which to call the Japanese planes. Male names would be attached to the Japanese fighter planes, and female names to the Japanese bombers. Thus the Zero, or Mitsubishi 1940 type low-winged monoplane fighter, came to be called "Zeke," and other fighters became Nate, Oscar, Rufe, Pete, Tony, and late in the war, one of the best Japanese fighters called, "Jack." The basic twin engine bomber was known as "Betty." (It was very *INTERESTING* to see some of the drawings of "Betty" (with twin engines) that the pilots sometimes drew when asked about her in a test, etc.) You had to have a little humor as you went along as this was very serious material . The dive bomber was Val, the four engine patrol plane, Emily, and other bombers were Lily, Sally and Nell.

Each of these planes had distinguishing characteristics, and that is what we, as teachers, had to learn (to perfection) in order to teach "Our Boys", as we called them. As I previously mentioned, all this was *BRAND NEW* to us so we never *WORKED HARDER* in our lives!!!! We were determined to be *GOOD* teachers and to know what we were talking about. I hope you will not take this as "bragging" but we were told *MANY* times how well we taught, how well we knew the material, and how well we conducted our classes.

In the Military, as a teacher in anything, you are one rank higher than the highest ranked officer in your class. This prevents anyone from trying to "throw their rank around". Our Officers were very polite, very understanding, very sharp, and really listened while in class. Once in a while we would have a very high ranking officer attend a class or two. We well recognized that he was in there to check on what type teaching we were doing and how well the Officers paid attention. We must have "filled the bill" as we were never replaced, never demoted, our teaching capabilities were asked for in several Squadrons, and we were often told that we knew more about recognition than anyone on the base. To this day I am most grateful, to God, for such an interesting, most unusual, dynamic and challenging position we had in the Corps.

I am very sure that the number of enlisted females that taught fighter pilots could be counted on both hands, if even that many. Fewer male enlisted did the same thing. We were really *fortunate* to be selected for such an interesting but exacting experience!!!

Our classes would be varied in size depending on many circumstances. Sometimes new groups would come on the base, sometimes our pilots would be called to active duty, sometimes some pilots would finish the basic numbers of hours required, etc. Very often even though a pilot had finished his required hours he would continue coming, as material kept changing all the time. Planes were either being added or deleted, as well as shipping tonnage, ships and submarines.

They wanted to be kept up to date. Because of all these changes our classes never became "dull"—everything was very dynamic and changing all the time. Whenever the Allies sank one of the Japanese ships, we had that ship immediately deleted from our syllabus. It almost was a "race" between our sharpest pilots and ourselves, as they would try to "catch us" with a sunken ship still on the syllabus. We were very determined to keep ahead of "Our Boys."

Many times we would have as many as 60-70 pilots, per hour. Often times the entire flight of five would attend class the same hour. We knew many of the Officers by name and many times we would be able to ask about a certain Officer, if he was not with his other flight members.

The F4U Vought Corsair had inverted gull-wings. When they first arrived in the southwest Pacific, the war began to change. It is said that a Japanese pilot, in a "Zero", came down and looked over the new plane with what amounted to undisguised curiosity. The Corsair could not only fly faster than any plane the Japanese possessed, but it could climb nearly 3,000 feet a minute!! It could go twice as far as the Navy's F4F. It was not long, at all, until the Corsairs gained aerial superiority over the Japanese fighters, and this superiority was never relinquished. Our pilots really *LOVED* their Corsairs!!

In the sixteen months that we taught our pilots, we had hundreds and hundreds of pilots go through our classes. To add a little "spice" to our class, on St. Patrick's Day we told our pilots that anyone who didn't "sign in" as "Irish" on that one particular day would not be recognized as having attended class that day. You should have seen all the "O's" and "Mc"s", that were added to their names that day.

Although we worked harder than we had ever worked in our lives, we also had many highly unusual and exhilarating experiences, due to our being Women Marines *and* being Instructors in Aircraft and Ship Recognition.

As we were about 40-45 miles from L. A. we often read about battleships, cruisers, or carriers coming into port in L. A. When we would read this we tried very hard to get the opportunity to visit these ships, if possible. We were never disappointed or refused to go aboard any ship that we went to see.

As I write this, so many years later, I can scarcely believe how easy it was to go aboard these ships, in wartime. Perhaps two Women Marines dressed in their "dress whites, walking in step, and handing out a little Irish "malarkey" helped a little. We were always welcomed aboard and given a full explanation of the ship, most often by the CO of the ship. This certainly made teaching about that particular ship all the more interesting, and dynamic, after having seen it in person.

We were fortunate to visit quite a few different ships; a battleship, a *CVE* (a small aircraft carrier), a cruiser, and we had dinner aboard the submarine, "Skate." The "Skate" had come into the harbor, at L. A. and was open for civilians to visit it during a big Bond Drive. The lines of people waiting to go aboard were very, very long. As we were Military we did not have to wait in those lines but were escorted to the head of the line and escorted aboard. It was a unique experience going aboard this submarine and feeling the close quarters once you were inside. As the afternoon progressed we were invited to stay and have evening "chow" with the submariners. I can now say that one of my pictures went "under the waves." I can also say "I would *not be a good submariner."*

These submariners were very proud of their ship's record, during the war. They had every right to be as the "Skate" had participated in many battles and had helped sink quite a few Japanese ships. They were also in the waters, very close to Japan, when the war ended. They were anticipating helping out with the invasion of Japan, but, thankfully, that did not become necessary.

the SHIP'S COMPANY
of the

UNITED STATES SUBMARINE

SKATE
(SS 305)

Lt. Comdr. John B. Dudley, Jr. USN—Commanding

WELCOMES YOU ABOARD

for

NAVY DAY

27 OCTOBER 1945
WILMINGTON, CALIFORNIA

A TRAUMATIC EVENT

One weekend in December, 1944, we had a traumatic experience. It was a very lovely weekend, weather wise, and we were feeling in the pink. This was during the time that we had to fast from midnight when one was preparing to receive Holy Communion the following day. We had gone to chow rather early on Saturday afternoon, and then to Confession Saturday evening.

Sunday we went to Mass and Holy Communion and then to early chow as we were hungry. The mess hall opened for Sunday dinner around 11 a. m. We had an exceptionally good dinner that particular sunny Sunday. To top off our delicious dinner, we had individually wrapped bars of ice cream, topped with some crushed pineapple.

We thoroughly enjoyed our early dinner, went back to our barracks, read the Sunday paper, visited with our friends, and then decided to go to our bunks and have a nap. "Irish" was on her top bunk and I on the bottom one when we were awakened by a very sudden illness. We were very sick to our stomachs and had to make many trips to the bathroom as long as we were able to feebly stumble in there. We soon became so weak, however, that we needed assistance to go to the bathroom and the hospital was contacted.

We didn't know it, but more and more Marine women, and men, were becoming ill. Soon all I can remember is being rolled off my bunk onto a gurney and taken to our base hospital. As so many new patients were being brought in from around the base, some of the patients who were already in the hospital had to be moved into the halls, etc. to accommodate the new patients.

I can barely remember being questioned, very soon after arriving at the hospital, about what I had eaten for dinner, etc. They were trying to discern the causal reason for the poisoning before people would be going to evening chow.

Finally the hospital was so full that our beds too, were out in a hall along one wall, head to head. I can just remember coming to enough to ask about how my sister was coming. We were having such retching that we were finally given some morphine to help us. We were in and out of consciousness for a couple days. We each lost several pounds.

At this same time we were up for promotion. We had to take a test for this promotion and if you did not take the test when it was given, you had to wait quite a while until you would have the opportunity again. We were in the hospital for a few days and we had told the Doctor about our dilemma. He told us we would not be well enough to write the test.

However, when the day came for the test we decided to stagger up to the building where we would take the test, without the permission of the hospital. I can still see us staggering along; anyone who observed us might have thought we had imbibed too heavily. We passed the test, went back to the hospital, from which we were legally discharged within the next day or two, and within a short period of time, made our promotion.

The final analysis of the problem was that we had had pineapple upside down cake for dessert on Saturday evening. Someone had neglected to take a big spoon out of a big, opened can of pineapple that was left over. The spoon had remained in the opened can all night, and on Sunday when the cooks were preparing Sunday dinner, they had opened several large cans of crushed pineapple and then had seen the pineapple left in the can from Saturday night and had put that pineapple in on the very top. The Marines who had eaten early on Sunday were the ones who had received the contaminated pineapple on our ice cream and were the ones who became ill. It was nothing short of a miracle that we did not have pineapple *sauce* as our dessert on Sunday or those of us who ate first would have eaten more of that contaminated pineapple and may not have survived.

Although it was not a laughing matter, my sister and I often remarked what a telegram that would have made, to our parents. informing them that their two daughters had been "killed in the mess hall."

This was only a one-time happening. We truly had excellent food in the Corps and were often very humbled to be eating so well when civilians, including our own family, and many in the other parts of the world were doing without so many things.

MOTHER'S ILLNESS

One afternoon shortly after we had begun teaching our Aircraft and Ship Recognition classes, we received a telegram through the American Red Cross that our dear Mother was seriously ill. She was out at our married sister's home back in Minnesota.

This news was extremely disturbing and upsetting to us. We immediately decided that we should get a leave and go home at once. We totally disregarded, in fact didn't even think about the chain of command, but early the next morning we called our Major Cotton and asked for permission to see her. She immediately granted this permission.

Major Cotton—the Women's Reserve "C.O."

Early in the morning here were two privates, standing at attention, in front of the desk of the C.O. of all the Women Marines at El Toro. She was not only a lovely person but a very attractive woman. In my mind's eye I can still see this setting. We immediately told her about receiving the telegram and that we strongly desired to be granted permission for a leave. To further emphasize the importance of our request I opened my big mouth by stating that if the Marine Corps didn't grant us the leave we would go *"AWOL."*

This sage statement could well have caused us great difficulty but she was very understanding and realized how traumatized we were by the news of the telegram.

She took it all very calmly and stated: "Well, privates, why don't we do this another way? Why don't one of you go home now, and if you see that your Mother is not improving, then we will allow the other one to also have a leave". How she calmed the troubled waters with this remark.

Eleanor went home and our brother Doc also came home from Richmond, California. This seemed to do the trick and Mother's health began to improve. It was not necessary for me to go home at that time.

We should have gone up the chain of command before going to talk to our Major, but anything wrong with either of our parents was a matter of major importance to us and nothing but going "right to the top" came to our mind, at that time. Even though my famous statement about going *"AWOL,"* could have gotten us into serious trouble everything turned out very well.

AN UNUSUAL EXPERIENCE

One weekend we were visiting Clare, in Los Angeles, when we three decided to do something unusual on Sunday afternoon. At that period of time, there was an Evangelical preacher by the name of Aimee Semple Mc Pherson. She had a very beautiful semi-circular, large, temple in downtown L.A. It was well publicized and was open for anyone to attend. It seemed to be the thing to do for many people at that time. This was many years ago and we were not too sure we should even attend but we thought it would be a unique experience and a once in a lifetime experience at that.

We decided to go. Inside the building there were several tiers of semi-circular seats all facing a stage, which she called the "altar." The building was large, beautiful and it was well filled. There were quite a few service people, with all the branches represented.

We sat quite high up.

Lo and behold, who should come in and sit right behind us but a young man from our small village of Dundee, Minnesota who had moved out to California several years before. He and I had been "competitors" in our class in our small town school. He was now married and living not too far out of L.A. What a coincidence to meet in this particular place.

This was our first experience of ever seeing an orchestra come up out of their pit. That made quite an indelible impression on us. But the best was yet to come. When the orchestra began playing, Aimee came "floating" down a long stairway, holding out the train on her white satin gown, carrying a huge bouquet of long stemmed, red roses. It was a spectacular sight. When she arrived on the stage, she gave a short talk, and then invited all the service personnel present to come down on the stage and receive one of the beautiful roses and a hand-signed copy of the New Testament.

We were in a dilemma. We felt that we really should not go but on the other hand we did not want anyone to think that Marines were not "cooperative", so we did go down. Once we were all assembled on the stage she gave a little talk about patriotism and then handed each of us one of her beautiful roses. One of her aides also gave each of us a small copy of the New Testament autographed by Aimee herself. It was a very unusual experience, but very nice and fondly remembered.

After a year or so went by, the L.A. papers had quite an article in them about Aimee's disappearance. It seemed that she is supposed to have gone out into the desert and disappeared. It was quite sensational and quite suspicious as to what really happened. To this day I don't know whether the truth has ever been found out!!!

BIRTH OF THE UNITED NATIONS

We went to visit" Doc" as often as we possibly could and he came to see us whenever he could have some free time. In 1945, we saw many articles in all the papers about a *BIG* meeting that was being held, in San Francisco, and how leaders from around the world were coming to try to formulate some type plan so we would have no further wars.

This was most intriguing to two former school teachers who were *VERY* interested in world events. We determined right away that that was something we would very much like to attend. We began formulating plans for a visit to Doc, and to attend as much of the conferences as we possibly could.

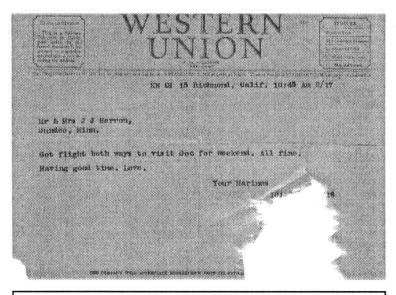

Visiting "Doc" in San Francisco

Our Lieutenant was on leave at that present moment so this delayed our getting permission to go, for a few days, until her return. She immediately sanctioned our leave and stated that she, too, would be very interested in attending those meetings. We contacted Doc, got our papers, obtained a flight, and away we went.

L to R: Eleanor, our brother, "Doc", Berneice and the "Packard Clipper". What fun we had!

The "Packard Clipper" with Eleanor in front and Berneice in the back. One of Doc's good friends owned this Packard.

We had a good time visiting Doc for a couple days and then we made our way into San Francisco to see about those famous U. N. meetings. We were informed as to where these meetings were being held, so we immediately got a taxi to take us there. The first place to go was into this one big building about two blocks from where the actual meetings were being held. These buildings were all cordoned off, with no one, except authorized personnel, to enter.

Irish and Mick on the way to the U.N. formation, in "forbidden" territory.

The first person we encountered was a very straight-laced middle-aged woman who, in no uncertain terms, informed us that we could go no further!!! We were/are very law-abiding citizens, but this was highly discouraging news and we knew she had no idea how interested we really were, nor how far we had come, just because of our realizing that what was going on here was on great significance. We stood outside that building, in the bright and beautiful sunshine and discussed what we should do.

We determined that we would go as far as the Military, who were on guard—ever so often, would allow us to go. We thought we would at least feel better to know we had given it our best "college try" and we also felt that if someone Military stopped us, that would be different. MP's (Army Military Police) and Navy S.P's (Navy Shore Patrol) were the guards stationed at check-points along the way. At first we approached the guards rather timidly, as we well knew we were not supposed to be in that area. All the guards were very friendly, about our age, and happy to have someone to talk to. After a little "Irish blarney" the guards would tell us that, as far as they were concerned, we could proceed and we did. The next guard would say that "far be it from him, to stop two Women Marines, etc". We kept proceeding until we were up to the building where the meetings were being held that day.

As we got closer to that building, we saw that there was an "Honor Guard" out in front, meeting all the stretch limousines that were arriving. We knew we had hit the jackpot.

As we approached, the service men, Army and Navy who comprised the Honor Guard, were all excited to see two Women Marines and immediately invited us to stand with them in the Honor Guard. We had really come a long way!!! We felt we shouldn't even be there, much less be part of the Honor Guard, but we were invited so why not participate?

So, from being warned not to venture any further than the first building we entered, here we now were, right beside the red carpet waiting for our first limousine to appear!. It didn't take long and a big limousine pulled up and out stepped Haile Selassie, from Ethiopia, in full regalia.

We all gave him our best salute and he quickly disappeared into the building. The Honor Guards told us who he was; they knew most of the Dignitaries as they had been doing this for some time.

The next limousine to arrive was carrying Molotov, from Russia. He too was dressed in his country's uniform; we gave him an extra "natty" salute, hoping to "soften" him up a bit. He even looked very "dour". It is very interesting, that in the letter home after this experience, I stated (over 60 years ago), that "we will have a lot of trouble, with Russia, before this is all over." How true that proved to be!

We fully realized that we had been told we weren't supposed to be, where we were, but being so close, we were determined to at least get our feet inside the building where these world famous meetings were being held. Our new Service friends highly encouraged us to do so. So, although the meetings being held at that time were "Secret" we gingerly approached the doorway to the building, and stepped inside.

Lo, and behold, who should be sitting, not that far away at a desk, but the *VERY SAME* woman who had told us, a couple blocks back, that we could go no further . We didn't stay long inside the building, but we also felt that if there was anyone who would appreciate the fact of being there, at that precise moment, more than we two Marines, she would have to look quite a ways to find them. At least we could honestly say all our lives that we HAD been in the building where the United Nations was being born.

Harold Stassen, a former governor of Minnesota, had served in the Navy as an aide to Admiral William Halsey. Stassen was a delegate to the formation of the U. N. and is the person who signed for the United States, on June 26, 1945. In the letter, previously mentioned, I also stated that I was afraid that "this big meeting isn't going to amount to much".

Besides fulfilling our great desire to attend these historic meetings, we thoroughly enjoyed our visit with our brother, Doc. Of course this was always helped along, as he had two special friends who thought he had a couple "pretty nice sisters," so they helped entertain us, whenever we were up there. One of them had just purchased a new "Packard Clipper", so we saw the entire area around San Francisco, danced to some of the Big Bands, ate in some of their fine restaurants, saw many good shows and always had a "super time."

We are *"THRILLED"* to have participated, in even such a small way, at the *"BIRTH OF THE UNITED NATIONS."*

Originally, only 90 nations were a part of the United Nations.

REHABILITATION INTERVIEWERS AND COLORADO SPRINGS

After V.J. Day, the main thrust of our teaching Aircraft Recognition and Ship Recognition, was over. Everyone was simply thrilled, beyond words, that the terrible war was finally over and that the Allies had won! Now the main objective for the Marines was to discharge the men, and women Marines, and to assist them in their Rehabilitation back into civilian life.

Eleanor and I were very interested in becoming Rehabilitation Interviewers, but at first it seemed that this was going to be done only by Marine Officers. However we were chosen to take a short course in this type work, and soon we were working as Rehabilitation Interviewers, at our beloved El Toro. At first we helped discharge Men Marines but soon we were working only in the area where we discharged Women Marines. In doing this type work, you interviewed the girls and helped them plan their future as civilians. We explained their rights and benefits, as civilians, and helped them with information regarding various colleges, etc. We also typed up their discharge papers. and explained the G. I. Bill of Rights.

There were only four discharge centers for the Marines—two on each Coast. One was at Washington, D.C, and one at Camp Lejeune, on the East Coast, and at San Diego, and El Toro, on the West Coast.

The requisites for being a Rehabilitation Interviewer were that you had to have some college work, some experience either in teaching, law, business, or personnel work, and that you had to be 25 years of age or older.

When we began our work, as Interviewers, we worked first in the Men's Discharge area. Soon, however, we were the two Women Interviewers and helped discharge the Women Marines from El Toro, San Francisco, and soon the gals came up from San Diego. I can't remember why they were not discharged down there. Anyway, we had a very busy schedule for quite some time.

It truly made us very sad to think that our own day of discharge was on the horizon. By mid-August, 1946 there were only 109 girls left at El Toro. Fifty of them were to be discharged on the 21st and the rest of us on August 22nd.

One weekend, shortly before this, we saw word on a bulletin board that some Colonel, from our Base, was going to fly to Colorado Spring, for the weekend and if any one had permission, to leave the Base, they could go with him. This sounded very appealing to us, so we obtained the proper permission and left our Base early on a Friday morning. We flew non-stop to Colorado Springs, but we had to fly way south to Santa Fe and come up on the east side of the mountains due to severe thunderstorms.

Even then we had fairly rough flying for a couple hours but arrived safely. When we arrived the Colonel was most gracious and said that we could accompany him, and his driver, into town. Once the Colonel arrived at his destination, he instructed the driver to take "the Marines" any place they wished to go.

Of course we had no reservations, so we asked the driver what the name of the best hotel was. He immediately replied, "The Antler's". We informed him to take us there.

Talk about confidence. Here were three Marine Staff-Sergeants stepping out of a chauffeur driven car, in front of a famous hotel, on a Friday afternoon in mid-August, and expecting to find a reservation! The long porch was filled with rocking chairs which were filled with very wealthy looking people, who, no doubt, had reservations made weeks, if not months, in advance, to stay there. They looked a little "perplexed" at the situation, but we strolled by them and into the lobby and up to the main desk.

Two younger men were working at the desk and as we came closer, we heard one say "My God, My Outfit, the Marines"!!! (We immediately knew we were "in".) When they found out we had no reservations, they disappeared to the back for a few moments, and they appeared asking us if part of the Bridal Suite would be O. K.? We told them that would suit us just fine, and what a *BEAUTIFUL SUITE* that proved to be, and what a beautiful view.

That evening we made arrangements to go on a very early morning trip to the top of "Pike's Peak" to see the sunrise from there. We left the hotel at 2 a. m.

Going up the mountain was no problem—it was dark, we were sleepy and didn't pay too much attention. It was a small, gravel, twisting and curving road and we were just about three miles high. Coming back down was another story. It was truly a once in a lifetime experience.

When we went to check out of the Antler's Hotel, we were told that our total bill, for the three of us, was $9.00. What a bargain and what a lovely time we had.

Saturday and Sunday nights we stayed with the WAC's who were part of the 15th Army Headquarters. They were very hospitable to us and we enjoyed our stay with them. On that Sunday, after Mass, we went on a tour to Manitou Springs, about seven miles from Colorado Springs. We visited the famous Broadmoor Hotel there. We had heard much about this hotel as another cousin of ours, Magdalen Proost, vacationed there several times.

Our flight back was very nice. Both ways we flew over the Grand Canyon, Painted Desert, Bryce Canyon, etc. It was all very thrilling and memorable. We arrived back on Base about 3 p. m. on that Monday. We were to have gone back on Sunday, but the Colonel called and said we weren't leaving until Monday; that was no problem for us. We couldn't be expected to return before the plane did.

OUR TRIP TO CATALINA ISLAND

Very late one week in 1946, we decided to take a boat and visit Catalina Island, about 20 miles off the coast of southern California. When we talked about it, a friend, Mary Jane Goodman, whom we all called "Goodie", said that she would like to accompany us. This was just fine as she was full of fun and had gone with us on some of our other adventures.

We found out rather late, that the boat leaving for Catalina left rather early and that we would not have time to go to Long Beach, on the bus. Dear Hank came to our rescue; we called him and he came over from Long Beach and picked us up. He had us over in Long Beach by 8:30 a. m. in time to catch the 9 o'clock boat. What a good friend Hank was.

There were about 1800 going over on the same boat as us—the Catalina. Smaller boats always come out to greet the incoming boats, as the passengers throw coins into the water and the ones on the smaller boats dive down in the beautiful Avalon Bay to retrieve them. The water is so clear that you can see the divers even when they are way down in the water.

Again we went to a very famous place, on a late Friday afternoon, just like we did when we went to Colorado Springs. Again, just because we were Military, we very extremely lucky to secure a lovely room in the Atwater Hotel just one block up from the beach. That afternoon we took a trip on Skyline Drive. We went past Zane Grey's home (we were told he wrote most of his western books, while on the island), past Gene Stratton Porter's home (another author) and saw the two Wrigley Estates.

Wrigley's owned most of the island except two square miles that they had leased to the town of Avalon. (They were the Wrigley's that owned so much of the gum). We also saw where the Chicago Cubs trained at that time.

The elder Mrs. Wrigley had a home way, way up on a cliff commanding a beautiful view of the entire bay. At night the mountains were all dark and from down in the town of Avalon it looked like her place, all lit up, was sitting on a cloud.

When we came back from our trip around the island, we decided to "take a nap", get up and put on our dress whites, have dinner, and then go to the 2 million dollar circular ballroom, the Avalon. Well, we had two double beds in our room and as our hotel was built into the side of a hill, our windows were relatively close to a sidewalk. "Irish" and I slept on our bed and "Goodie" laid down on hers. It was all meant to be a couple hours nap, at the most. None of us had taken our wrist watches with us, as this was to be leisurely weekend, and one without having to watch the time.

We all went fast asleep and one of us was awakened by voices coming in our window, saying "Well, good night—good night, etc." The streetlights were shining in our windows. We called down to the desk to inquire about the time. We were informed that it was one in the morning! What a nap. We had slept right through dinner time and had completely missed out on a night of much desired dancing in the famous ballroom.

Irish and I could understand how we, being "champion" sleepers, could have done this, but we were very surprised about "Goodie." Anyway, we had some food delivered to our room, went back to bed, and woke up early on Saturday morning.

Saturday we really had a big day. We seemed to be some of the very few who wore many clothes. Most every one lived in their bathing suits, or sun suits. It was interesting for us to note, too, that the majority of visitors on the island were older people. This had also been true in Colorado Springs. We were happy to see this and hoped that, some day, we would be able to bring our parents out to visit here, also.

Saturday evening we dressed up in our dress whites. As always, they really were highly complimented. We *LOVED* those uniforms!! What fun we had, dancing, on Saturday night!!! What a place that was and what lighting they had.

On Sunday we went to Mass, had a good dinner, and then walked around, took pictures, visited with many people, and looked at all the beautiful cruisers, and ships, that were in the harbor there.

We had to catch the 4:30 boat back to shore and were back at our base at 9 p.m. What a wonderful 71 hr. pass that had been. It made another indelible memory.

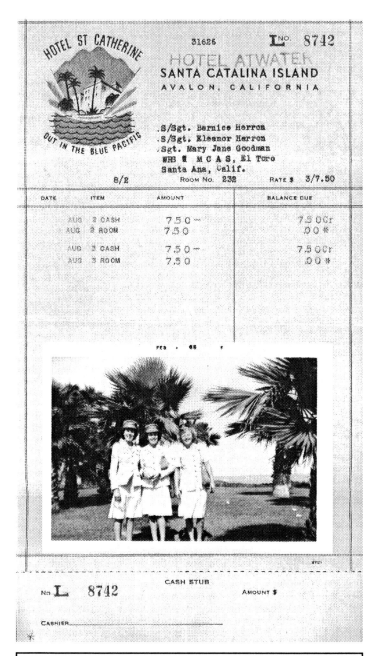

Irish, Mick and "Goodie" on a 71 hr. pass to Catalina Island.

VJ DAY CELEBRATION and PATTON—DOOLITTLE PARADE

After the cessation of the hostilities of WWII, the Allies had much to rejoice about. Many celebrations, parades, and other events took place in cities, small towns and villages. Everyone was rejoicing that the terrible fighting had finally come to an end and that the Allies had been victorious!! Every man, woman, and child had contributed his/her best efforts to win the war and now was a time for celebration. Emotions ran high!! Troops were coming home!!! Loved ones were being reunited!!!

I, for one, will *NEVER* forget the *JOYOUS, EXCITING and MEMORABLE,* "V. J." celebration in Los Angeles!!! All Marines were confined to Base, for "V.E" night, but there was no holding them back on "V. J." night!!!!! Not after what *THEY* had been through to make this Victory really happen!! There were *THRONGS* of all Branches of the Service present. What "pent up emotions", excitement and pure joy were evident!!! Bells were ringing, ships were blowing their horns, bands were playing, people were dancing in the streets, bonfires were lit, people were banging anything they could that made a noise, there was singing, crying, laughing, enormous crowds meeting on the corners of the street, hugging, kissing, and everyone nearly delirious with joy!!! It was a night so full of sounds and sights that it is indelibly imprinted on my psyche!!!

For weeks, and weeks, the Los Angeles, and other papers were filled with information talking about the *BIG* parade that would soon be coming, in L.A., for General Patton and Brigadier General James Doolittle. Planes were being sent out about two hundred miles to meet their incoming planes. It was to be a celebration of great importance, and meaning.

Brigadier General James Doolittle, on April 18, 1942, led the Bomber attack of sixteen B-25's called the "Tokyo Raid." This was the first bombing strike on Japan and was a signal, to them, that their cities were within striking distance of the Americans!! This proved to be quite a shock to them!! He was awarded the Congressional Medal of Honor for this, and was promoted from Lieutenant

Colonel to Brigadier General, by-passing Colonel. He later commanded U. S. Army Air Force Units in North Africa and Europe.

General Patton was nicknamed "Blood and Guts" and was well known for his equestrian ability. He commanded the U. S. Third Army in the fighting across Europe and died as a result of injuries in a postwar auto accident and is buried at Diekirch, Luxembourg. (l945). Loving history, as we both did/do, we planned to be present at this parade, if humanly possible. We were thrilled to read that it was to be held in L.A. We were very fortunate to obtain a 48 hr. pass, and into Long Beach we went.

The day of the parade was a bright, sunny Saturday. We went into Los Angeles and were right at curbside, when the parade came up the street. There were several bands and then came Patton's part. He was standing in the very first jeep and had a big bouquet of red roses. With the exception of the flowers, he looked every bit the way he had always looked in the pictures we had seen.

He had on his helmet, two pistols on his hips, and he had on his boots. When he went past the place where we were standing he tossed one of his roses and said "For the Marines." The rose fell out in the street; a young boy, standing near ran out and got it. His mother made him give it to us as she had heard what the General had said.

Many jeeps followed Patton's. Other two star Generals, Majors, etc. were also being honored. They had all been part of Patton's Army, in Europe. Brigadier General Doolittle followed in the 25th jeep. He, too, was followed by many of his Officers, who, too, were being honored. It was a very long and interesting parade, but the best was to come that night in the Los Angeles Coliseum. *THAT* was *SPECTACULAR.*

The crowd was *HUGE.* There were Movie Stars galore!! We arrived at the Coliseum, early, and they seated us in the Purple Heart section. What a super place and what an honor to be seated there.

Jack Benny was the Master of Ceremonies. Bette Davis, Judy Garland, Jimmy Durante, Jeanette McDonald, and many others were in attendance. The program, lighting and all were perfect. At one intense moment a lone "B-25" flew over the Coliseum (Doolittle's first plane over Japan) followed by five "B-29's" (the planes that were over Tokyo at that very time.) Was that ever thrilling!!!! Then they had the land in the center of the Coliseum all filled with something to represent land mines. When they went off five big Army tanks came in "shooting" their guns and roaring—all symbolic of Patton's tank divisions. Talk about "fireworks, loud banging and explosions."

All of this excitement, plus the acts put on by the Movie Starts, plus being in the "Purple Heart" section, made for a truly once-in-a-lifetime experience. It is as vivid in my mind, today, as if it just took place. How fortunate we were to be able to attend such an historic event!

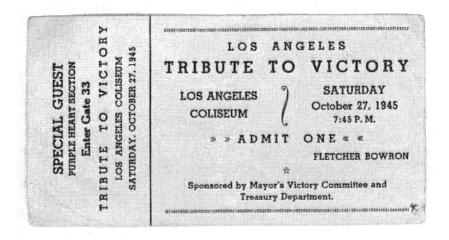

Ticket to Patton-Doolittle Celebration in Los Angeles, CA, 1945

OUR SEPARATION PARTY

The next big excitement would be our big Separation Party that the Corps was planning for the Women Marines. It was going to be held on the evening of August 14th and at the famous, "Tom Breneman's", in Hollywood. Each Lady Marine could invite a date, and some additional invitations were offered to some of the First Marine Wing that had just returned to our Base after nearly four years of very difficult combat.

After their years of some of the fiercest fighting in the southwest Pacific, they had just recently been in China, to help maintain order there between two fighting Chinese factions. All these Marines were very "salty". They had been in the war for a long time and had many decorations including campaign bars, hash marks and other type decorations.

One that I met was going to be 26 years of age that June and he had been in the Marines nearly 8 years, having enlisted on his 18th birthday. He had served all over the Pacific and was one of the original "Carlson's Raiders." These men had fought the Japanese from island, to island, in the Pacific. When the war began they were all young, inexperienced and not used to jungle warfare. They were up against the most experienced, biggest and best trained of the Japanese troops. What bravery, sacrifice and traumatic experiences they all shared!!

Eventually the "Carlson Raiders" sent a company of their men back to the States to organize and train the "Edson Raiders." These two groups of Raiders were some of the best known and courageous combatants of the entire war. To have been a member of either of these groups and to have lived to tell about it was nothing short of a miracle!!

As the time of the Separation Party approached all the male Marines really "banged ears" to receive an invitation. Photographers from both the "Look" and "Life" magazines were there, as well as photographers from our own station.

Buses came from Los Angeles to furnish transportation for anyone who did not have any other way to get to Hollywood. The party started at seven o'clock, dinner at 8:30 and two orchestras furnished the music for dancing.

What a wonderful, fun party!!! Excellent food and cocktails, superb music, dancing with many wonderful dancers, good conversation, many laughs, and super memories.

The party was one wonderful way to say "thank you" to all the Women Marines who had done such wonderful work in the Corps! Quite a few dignitaries attended our party including the greatest "Ace" of all the Marine Corps Aces, Gregory "Pappy" Boyington, who is credited with shooting down a total of 28 Japanese planes!!!

The Marine Corps had taken over Tom Breneman's night club for this party. It was in the heart of Hollywood. Each Woman Marine was given several pictures of her party and a lovely gift. It was truly a night to remember, and has never been forgotten.

Mick, Irish and friends at the Separation Party. What a party!. Good friends, good food, good conversation and "great fun" dancing.

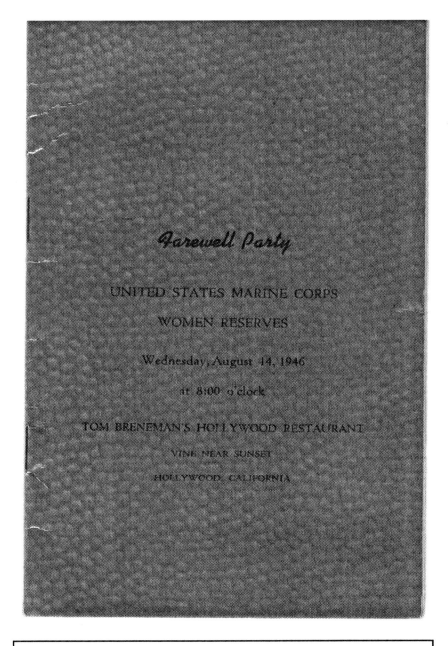

The special invitation to the Separation Party.

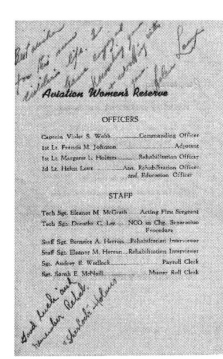

Inside the invitation to the Separation Party.

THE CALIFORNIANS

I would be very remiss if I did not write about the goodness, of the people of California, during the WWII years. I cannot speak for them, today, but I wish to tell you, a little, about many/most of them, that we Service people met, during our days of Service, in their beautiful state.

To begin with, California was saturated with Bases, of all Branches of the service. They also absorbed hundreds, and hundreds, of Navy personnel as so many ships came into port, there.

The "Natives" never seemed to be overwhelmed. They opened their homes, and their hearts, to many a lonely service person, far away from their home. Many holidays, as well as many other times, found hundreds of young men, and women, being royally entertained by "regular folks."

They made sandwiches, cake, cookies, coffee, etc. for days, on end, and then willingly, and happily, served in the Canteens, and Guest Houses, for the Service people, all out of the goodness of their hearts.

Many times they would take "hitch hikers" quite a few miles, extra, to get them to their desired destinations. Very few ever passed by a "hitch hiker." Hitch hiking was very safe, in those days, and most all service personnel, both male, and female, got many free rides by just standing by the side of the road. Often drivers would take you to your destination, if it was not *too far away.*

Very often Service personnel were given "free tickets" to many outstanding events.

This is just a "sampling" of the many courtesies we all experienced. The residents were simply *"GREAT.* They simply could not have done more.

I am sure I speak for thousands, and thousands, of "G.I's, when I say "Thank you, thank you, and may God bless those, who are still living, and those who are deceased." Their goodness is indelibly imprinted in our hearts, and we will never forget them, and their great acts of kindness.

Berneice

A NOTE TO ALL READERS

In the many hours I have spent, in writing, and re-writing this book, I have come to realize that our family represented the four main categories of citizens, in the U.S.A. that fought, and won, that long, hard war.

My dear parents, Joseph James and Mary Lillian Herron, represented millions of parents who saw their sons, and daughters, off to war and quietly, patiently and prayerfully hoped for the best and eagerly looked forward to receiving word that their loved one/s were O.K. They also bought the Bonds that helped finance the war, raised the Victory Gardens, worked in Defense, kept the Home Fires Burning, and helped their neighbors. Most importantly, they went to their house of worship and prayed for the safety of their loved ones, and all others. They constituted the very "backbone" of our society and their contributions were of immense importance in winning the war.

My brother, Joseph Donald Herron, (Doc) represented the thousands, and thousands, who through no fault of their own, were unable to go into the military, but would have loved to have done so. Many times snide remarks were made about these men, and that made things even worse. Many times these men did very valuable civilian work that also was extremely necessary in the total war effort. Doc helped work on the famous and very necessary "Liberty Ships." Without their fast construction our country would have been unable to get military personnel, food, ammunition, and other necessities to essential localities. He was one, out of many, who helped in ways other than being military.

My sister, Eleanor Margaret, and I, Berneice Ann, were on actual duty in the Military. We represented millions of men, and women, who left good jobs and homes, and went to "far away places" and to very strange lands to fight for our American way of life and for our freedoms, and liberty. Many thousands, of our generation, gave their life fighting for their homes, and families The wives, and children, of many of our service personnel are not to be forgotten for the sacrifices they all made in so many, and varied ways.

My married sister, Alice Mercedes, and husband, Vincent Brennan, represent the fourth category of citizen. They were the hard working, industrious, law abiding, and younger farmers who conscientiously worked the soil and raised the immense amount of food to keep the military, and everyone else, so well fed. They also furnished the many hours of volunteerism in many capacities. They often looked after their older parents which greatly relieved the siblings who were in uniform. I fully realize this was the case in our family. I am forever grateful for all they did in my sister's, and my absence. They made a lonesome and sad time tolerable, by their goodness and presence, when the "chips were down" or illness struck. They very often did *MORE* than their fair share in whatever needed to be done, for either set of parents.

I am sure there were thousands, and thousands, just like them. They deserve/d many more accolades than they received. They were our "unsung heroes and heroines".

A DREAM

I always felt that our Marine Corps Days should be made into a book. I also knew this would take much work, time and expense. It was something that I thought about, but always seemed to have a good excuse for not getting started.

We were sworn into the Corps on December 14, 1943 and were discharged on August 22, 1946. We left, for Boot Camp from Los Angeles, and were discharged at the Marine Corps Station, at El Toro, out of Santa Ana, California. During the two years 8 ½ months we were in the Corps, we wrote home, to our parents ALMOST every day!! We did miss a few, but not very many. Because we wrote so often, we sometimes wrote only a postcard, or a very short letter. Some of these were handwritten, but most of them were typewritten. Sometimes one of us would begin the letter and then the other would finish it.

Our dear mother kept all these letters, cards, pictures, etc. in a big suitcase. Mother told us that she would read, and reread each letter; until a new one came along .We know well that she missed us terribly and was very lonesome without us being closer by. Our town, Dundee, Minnesota, was very small (around 225 people—at best) and many of these were gone, either into the Service, or working in Defense. It was a very quiet and lonesome time, and place. Not too many families had two daughters in the Service. She, as well as our Dad, when he returned from California, really looked forward to these letters!!

As the years progressed many of the letters were separated from their envelopes. As we wrote so often, many times we did not put the exact date on the letter, but only wrote the name of the weekday, etc. About once a year, Eleanor and I would get out these letters and read, and reread, some of them. Then we decided that we should, at least, try to put them into some type order, so we separated them, by years—1943-44-etc. We put them into large Manila envelopes and back into a smaller suitcase.

Not long ago, our only niece, Janyce Hanish, came to visit from New Bern, N.C. She read, and re-read, some of the letters and was very adamant that they were "historical" and should be preserved! She insisted that we obtain "folders with plastic sleeves" and get those letters in order. She took a big number of them home with her and arranged them beautifully. I did the others. Now they are like a "diary" of those interesting, dynamic, and historical years.

It is the fact that I have those letters, which prompted me to begin thinking about writing, "My Memoirs" in late September, 2005. My question was, "How am I going to do this?"

Many of my friends had purchased computers several years ago. I did not buy one at first, as I felt I would have to rearrange my apartment to accommodate one, and I did not feel I wanted to do that. But now, I felt that in order to write "My Memoirs", I would need to obtain one. In March 2005, my grandnephew Sean Brennan, helped me order my streamlined, 17", Dell Computer. I did not know how to turn it on when I ordered it, but I felt that once I had it, I would be forced to learn. That has been the situation.

I do not know too many functions of my computer, but I am very happy with what I have been able to accomplish. I *love* my computer and wish I had purchased one before.

When Janyce sent her completed notebook back, from New Bern, she also wrote a note. She stated that she had thought, and thought, about a good name for this "project". She thought of humorous names, Marine Corps names, and when she reread some of the letters, again, she realized that 95% of them started out with the salutation, "Dearest Folks", so she thought that should be the title. I couldn't be more pleased, and it couldn't be more "fitting" as that is definitely to whom these letters had been written. She named the "Memoirs". That is why the formal title is, "DEAREST FOLKS".

A MESSAGE FROM THE COMMANDANT

To each of you "Goodbye"

For a Job Well Done

"My Grateful Thanks"

For a Happy Future

"My Sincere Hopes"

                A.A. Vandergrift
                Commandant, U.S. Marine Corps

MY NINETIETH BIRTHDAY

It always seems that it will happen to other people, but not to you. However the day does come and all of a sudden you are 90 years of age. This was what happened to me on March 4, 2006. From that beginning, back on the farm, outside of the small village of Dundee, Minnesota, here I am 90 years later living in Florida, where I have resided for the past 25 years.

I spent 47 of my years either going to school, teaching in rural and small town schools, teaching in the Marine Corps, and then the last 27 of my working years as a school social worker in the St. Paul, Minnesota, public schools.

During all this time my sister, Eleanor, and I did extensive traveling, by car, airplanes, cruise ships and "freighters." We loved to travel, see new places, experience other cultures and meet people. Our philosophy has always been that "People matter most." We loved to meet people from other cultures and from other parts of the world.

We have an "adopted" daughter, and family, from Vietnam, a very dear Archbishop friend, Archbishop Lawrence Khai, from Thailand, and a "Godson," Joseph Jagod, whose mother is Filipino.

For quite a few years we belonged to the "International Center" at the University of Minnesota, and through them we have entertained people for *MANY* areas of the world. We loved being "citizen diplomats."

We have also entertained many groups in our home so that they could meet visiting Missionaries, from several countries, including the world famous "Noodle Priest". from Hong Kong. He came, several times, to meet with the big flour milling companies, in the Twin Cities, and then we would have him to our home, and have our friends in to meet him. We had the most dynamic, unusual, and interesting experiences, two different holiday times, handing out "noodles" to the Chinese Refugees, in Hong Kong. That is where we met Monsignor John Romaniello, the "noodle priest" We went to Hong Kong both of the years that we taught in the Philippines.

For my birthday my only niece, Janyce Maree Brennan, drove from New Bern, No Carolina, and spent two weeks with me. Her brother, my only nephew, Gerald Joseph Brennan, (Jerry), and his wife, Veronica (Ronnie), drove down from Dover, Delaware, and one of their sons, Michael (Mike) flew down from Rutherford, New Jersey. His wife, Colleen, had planned to come, also, but because of her heavy work schedule was unable to do so. Jerry and Ronnie's youngest son, Sean, now lives in Tampa and is the one who has helped me with my book.

Family members present for my 90th birthday, March 4, 2006.
L to R: Michael Brennan, grandnephew, Rutherford, NJ, Janyce Maree Hanish, only niece, New Bern, NC, Berneice Herron (author), Veronica (Ronnie) Brennan, nephew's wife, Dover, DE, Sean Brennan, grandnephew, Tampa, FL

On right: Gerald Joseph Brennan (Jerry), only nephew, Dover, DE

Also present: Lisa Lan Thai, my adopted Vietnamese daughter, Eagan, MN.

My "adopted" daughter, Lisa Lan Thai, and a friend, flew down from Eagan, Minnesota. A couple of other friends, Bill and Mary Mulvihill, from Farmington, Minnesota also flew down. What a good time we had.

Berneice with some of her 90th Birthday cards.

I cannot express how thankful and happy I was to see them all and to have such lovely parties and such delicious food, cakes, flowers, cards, gifts, etc. I was totally overwhelmed with all the cards, too, that I received from all my friends. I don't believe that too many people can write about their 90th birthday in a book that they are just having published.

I am most fortunate and most grateful.

Berneice Herron.

EPILOGUE

After we returned home, from having been in the Marines, we went back to Mankato State Teacher's College and received our Bachelor's Degrees in Education. That G.I. Bill of Rights" was like "Manna from Heaven." It helped so many GI's better their education and their life. They were then able to pay back so much more in taxes that that bill was paid for in a very short span of time. It has been considered one of the best pieces of legislation ever offered, and I, for one, surely agree.

As we continued in our educational careers, Eleanor received two Master's degrees and I received my Specialist Degree which is a degree between the Master's and the Doctorate. We were both fortunate to receive many awards during our careers—Eleanor was nominated for "Minnesota Teacher of the Year", and received a plaque from the University of Minnesota, in l969, designating her as "Education Alumni Member of the Year." I was most surprised, and honored, to be included in the "Fifth Edition of the l968-69 "Who's Who of American Women."

In furthering our education, Eleanor and I attended the University of Minnesota and I received my Specialist Degree from St. Thomas College, in St. Paul, Mn. We also took courses in Boulder, Colorado, Washington, D, C. and we took many night classes, weekend classes, seminars, workshops, etc. We both loved to go to college, so this was no problem for either of us.

From l961 to l963 we both took a leave of absence from our positions in the St. Paul Public Schools and went with the Department of Defense, to the Philippines, where Eleanor taught in both the sixth and seventh grades, and where I started the first school social work program for the Overseas Schools. We loved the Filipino people and their most beautiful country. We were most fortunate to be able to travel from one end of their country to the other in the two years we were there.

We felt a special attachment to the Philippines as many of the Pilots we had instructed, during our Marine Corps Days, were stationed here. It was in the

Philippines, too, that the very infamous Bataan Death March had occurred. It was also here, that the American and Filipino military were so starved, and extremely cruelly treated at the infamous prison camp, Cabanatuan.

We had the privilege to take a bus ride up the Bataan Peninsula and it certainly made us more aware of how traumatic, brutal, and savage our combined American and Filipino forces were treated. Thousands never made it and those who did were put into box-cars for the last part of their journey before being incarcerated in prison camps that defied description.

We looked for homes, in California and Texas before deciding to move to Sun City Center, Florida, in 1981. We purchased a home and lived, happily, in it until 1995. Our brother, "Doc" lived with us there until his death in November, 1984.

Our married sister, Mercedes, and her husband, Vincent Brennan, moved to Plant City, Florida, in late 1983 and we had many happy times together, before Vincent's death in 1984 and Mercedes' death, in November, 1985. (We lost the three of them within a 16 month period.) They are all buried in the Mansion Memorial Park, in Ellenton, as is Eleanor, who passed away on February 1, 1998.

In 1995 Eleanor and I sold our home to our only niece, Janyce Maree (Brennan) Hanish, and husband, Robert, and we moved into the retirement home, Lake Towers, now renamed Sun Towers, where I currently live. It is located in Sun City Center, Florida.

Janyce and husband, Robert, sold our home, here in Sun City Center, after 4 years, and moved into a new home in New Bern, North Carolina, where they currently reside. It is interesting that they are now living very close to Camp Lejeune, where Eleanor and I went to Boot Camp.

Our only nephew, Gerald Joseph Brennan (Jerry) and wife, Veronica (Ronnie), lived for many years in North Arlington, New Jersey, where they raised their three sons, Pat, Mike, and Sean. About two years ago, shortly before Christmas they, too, moved into a new home, in Dover, Delaware. Jerry and Ronnie's youngest son, Sean, is now employed at the Art Institute of Tampa as one of their Academic Department Directors. He lives about 40 miles from me, and is my "advisor" in using my computer and in writing "My Memoirs," His specialty is "Graphic Design."

I am most grateful, to God, for a very long, interesting and exciting life. I have been blessed with extremely good health—at least for the first nearly ninety years of my life. I do not know what the future holds in store, for me. I thank God, daily, for all his graces, and blessings.

I decided to write up these interesting years, but they were not the only ones I could have written about. Eleanor and I traveled, all over, mostly by car, for 55 years, or more. We had many trips, also by air, by "Freighter", and by boat. We visited nearly all the Catholic shrines—Medjugorje, Guadalupe, Lourdes, St.Ann's, etc. We were very instrumental in helping our parish, in St. Paul; adopt a Vietnamese family, in 1975. We belonged, for years, to the "International Center" at the University of Minnesota, and through them we entertained many students, guests and "V.I.P's in our home. We thought that we could be "Citizen Diplomats" and this proved to be *EXTREMELY* interesting, as well as educational, for us, and we hope we helped show our guests how average Americans live. We surely answered many questions, and made many very interesting friends!!!!

I am very grateful that I have been able to write about, most of the interesting things that happened to us while in the Marine Corps. I wrote it, in large part for my own gratification, but also for my family, and friends, who know we were in the Corps, but who did not have much more information about what all we actually did. I do hope it proves to be interesting reading for anyone who takes the time, and effort, to read it.

SEMPER FI!!

PHOTOS FROM THE EARLY YEARS

Irish and Mick with parachutes.

On a trip.

Irish "Goodie" and Mick

Bing gave all of us a "great" performance that night. He was super!

Irish teaching her "Boys".

Mick on holiday at Big Bear, in the San Bernadino Mts. about 7,000' elevation.

We talked to Keye Lukes at the Canteen. He used to be the "son" in the Charlie Chan movies.

L to R: Eleanor Herron, 2nd Lt., Helen Loux, 1st Lt., Margaret Holmes and Berneice Herron

Women's Separation Center Personnel at El Toro, CA.

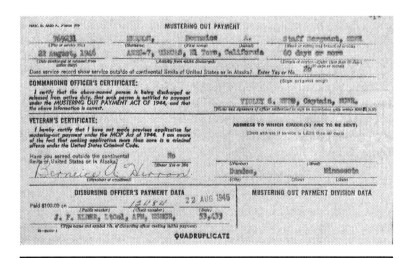

Mustering out payment

```
              AVIATION WOMEN'S RESERVE SQUADRON NINE
                      MARINE AIR WEST COAST
         MARINE CORPS AIR STATION, EL TORO, (SANTA ANA), CALIF.

MAWC11/P17-2                                          12 June 1946
BS:emw

SQUADRON PROMOTION ORDER )
                         :
NUMBER        17-1946    )

References:    (a) Ltr of Instn 1216 dtd 17Jan46.
               (b) ALMAR-19 dtd 14Feb46.

     1.     In accordance with the authority granted in ref-
erences (a) and (b), the following promotions are effective this
date:

               TO STAFF SERGEANT, "AVIATION DUTY" TEMPORARY:

               HERRON, Berneice A.      Sgt      (769231)
               HERRON, Eleanor M.       Sgt      (769232)

               TO SERGEANT, "AVIATION DUTY" TEMPORARY:

               GOODMAN, Mary J.         Corp     (757911)
               HUTCHINS, Elizabeth      Corp     (753976)

               TO CORPORAL, "AVIATION DUTY" TEMPORARY:

               RAND, Amy D.                      (771726)
               STARINA, Eleanor                  (772740)

     2.     For the purpose of seniority, the date of rank
of this promotion will be shown as 12 June 1946.


                              B. SOMERS
                         Captain, U. S. Marine Corps Reserve
                                Commanding Officer

Copy:   CMC; DofA; StaPM; StaDisp; CG, MAWG; Dep Chief of Staff;
        MAWG; PMO; Wash, D. C.; Each person concerned; F I L E.
```

Promotion Roster

1355-40
DDA-483-hdk

HEADQUARTERS U. S. MARINE CORPS
WASHINGTON 25

16 October 1945

From: Commandant of the Marine Corps.
To: All Commanding Officers within the continental limits of the United States; the Commanding General, Marine Garrison Forces, Fourteenth Naval District; and the Commanding Officer, U. S. Marine Corps Air Station, Ewa, T. H.

Subject: The Marine Corps Women's Reserve, services of.

1. Officers and enlisted personnel of the Marine Corps Women's Reserve are now being rapidly separated from the service because of the fact that the entire Women's Reserve is to be demobilized by 1 September 1946.

2. It was with some hesitation that the Marine Corps admitted women to its ranks in February, 1943; but during the intervening years they have made a most valuable contribution to the Corps. They can now be found in key positions connected with administration, training, and supply at Marine Corps posts and stations all over the United States and in Hawaii. As the time comes to release them, I am reminded again of the important part they have played in support of our combat Marines while the actual fighting was in progress.

3. Many of the women reservists are now playing an equally important part in hastening the return home of these same combat Marines. They hold responsible positions in the demobilization system and have become skilled in the administrative procedures necessary to speed discharges. I feel sure that enough of them will remain at these posts to keep the demobilization process running smoothly.

4. I wish to express to the members of the Women's Reserve the appreciation of the Marine Corps for the valuable contribution they have made to its success. They have performed their duties in a manner that evokes the admiration and praise of their fellow Marines; and their conduct and appearance, both on and off duty, have been exemplary and a source of pride to us all.

5. Please convey this message to the members of the Marine Corps Women's Reserve under your command.

A. A. VANDEGRIFT

TEACHING MATERIALS

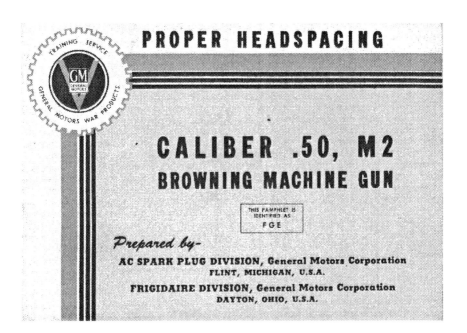

Op-33-D1
CONFIDENTIAL

NAVY DEPARTMENT
OFFICE OF THE CHIEF OF NAVAL OPERATIONS
WASHINGTON 25, D. C.

M E M O R A N D U M

15 September 1944

From: Op-33-D1.

To: Staff Recognition Officers.

Subject: "SUBS DO HAVE RECOGNITION FEATURES"

1. In the November issue of "The Recognition Journal" an article dealing with submarine recognition will appear. The purpose of this memorandum is to not only outline the substance of the article, but to give you additional information which is classified as confidential and hence not to be mentioned in the Journal article.

2. This office has conferred with COMINCH staff officers about this problem of submarine recognition. There is a very definite place for recognition in this difficult identification problem. We quote a source from Tenth Fleet (Naval Aviator)--"In frontier waters where both friendly and enemy submarines operate, pilots are quite often confronted with one of the nastiest recognition problems in the book--that of determining the nationality of a submarine in the brief interval between sighting and diving. Positive plane-to-submarine recognition is unusually difficult because subs, unlike surface craft, do not sit and wait for recognition. Under-sea boats, regardless of nationality, have the disconcerting habit of ducking before recognition--or an attack can be made. Officially, the onus of identification rests with the submarine. Pilots, however, can't very well go steaming around taking pot-shots at every submarine sighted.

"There are numerous ways and means established to aid both the submarine and the plane in this recognition problem. Proper briefing on sub positions, bomb restriction areas and sanctuaries, proper use of identification and recognition signals, radio, radar and mechanical aids--all are designed to prevent mistakes being made.

"With all of these, however, a pilot may still possibly find himself in the proverbial pickle--a submarine sighted outside restricted areas but close to a friendly sub position. The approach is started, no identification signals are seen, everything is legal for the drop, and yet enough friendly-enemy doubt remains to ruin the attack."

RESTRICTED

SH-3AR   NAVAER 00-25Q-13

MODEL DESIGNATION
OF
NAVAL AIRCRAFT

APRIL 1945

NAVY DEPARTMENT
BUREAU OF AERONAUTICS
WASHINGTON

CONFIDENTIAL   JUNE 1945
OPNAV-16-V#T 304

10262

REPRESENTATIVE ENEMY AND ALLIED AIRCRAFT

COMPARATIVE PERFORMANCE AND CHARACTERISTICS
TAIC MANUAL NO. 2
THIRD EDITION

Issued in the Division of Naval Intelligence
By
Combined Personnel of United States and British Services
for the Use of Allied Forces

TECHNICAL AIR INTELLIGENCE CENTER
NAVAL AIR STATION   ANACOSTIA D C

NOT TO BE TAKEN INTO THE AIR

769231
DSL-1183-alm

STATEMENT OF MARINE CORPS TRAINING OF
BERNEICE ANN HERRON, (769231)MCWR

1. Enlisted: December 15, 1943, at Los Angeles, California.

2. Basic Training: From February 23, 1944, to April 4, 1944, at Recruit Depot, Marine Corps Women's Reserve Schools, Camp Lejeune, North Carolina.

    REFERENCE: Section 3, Institutional Policies, Page B-1.00.

3. Promotions: To Private First Class on September 1, 1944.
To Corporal on January 11, 1945.
To Sergeant on February 12, 1946.
To Staff Sergeant on June 12, 1946.

4. Training Completed: SYNTHETIC TRAINING COURSE, Gunnery School, Marine Corps Air Station, Cherry Point, North Carolina. Satisfactorily completed the course of instruction on July 4, 1944.

    REFERENCE: Section M.C. 2, C(1)2, Page S-96,87.

NOTE: References are to the handbook, "A Guide to the Evaluation of Educational Experiences in the Armed Services", and indicate the pages on which course description and recommended credit may be found. Copies may be purchased from the American Council on Education, 744 Jackson Place, N. W., Washington 6, D. C.

5. Military Duties: OCCUPATIONAL TECHNICIAN: Assists Marines in vocational and educational problems involved in their separation from military service. Studies individual cases and performs such services as analyzing experience and aptitudes and interpreting test results. Recommends suitable fields for civilian employment, and refers Marines to proper civilian agencies for employment services.
    Must be thoroughly familiar with personnel classification procedures, military and civilian occupations for various jobs, and opportunities for employment.

RECOGNITION INSTRUCTOR: Instructs personnel in the recognition of all types of friendly and enemy air and surface craft by distinguishing markings, silhouettes, sounds of motors, and construction. May use still or motion pictures as training aids.
    Must be thoroughly familiar with all methods of identifying air and surface craft.

Women's Reserve Employment

At the end of the war a statistical breakdown of the 17,672 women on duty on 1 June 1945 showed them working in the following occupations:

Professional; Semi-professional

Scientific	76
Personnel	338
Artistic, Musical	306
Misc (teachers)	622
TOTAL	1,342

Clerical

Clerk General	1,764
Clerk Typist	2,982
Stenographer	1,129
Special Clerical	1,182
Clerical: Supervisory or Administrative	498
Clerical: Communications	661
Clerical: Supply	1,936
Clerical: Office Machine Operators	127
TOTAL	10,279

Sales

TOTAL	741

Service

Personal Service	438
Protective Service	149
TOTAL	587

Mechanical

Mechanical: Aviation	1,086
Mechanical: Non-Aviation	285
TOTAL	1,371

Skilled Trades

Skilled Trades Aviation	83
Skilled Trades Non-Aviation	261
TOTAL	344

Semi-Skilled Jobs

Semi-skilled: Aviation	143
Semi-skilled: Non-Aviation	1,162
TOTAL	1,305

Unskilled Jobs

TOTAL	14

Students

TOTAL	35

General Duty: not elsewhere classified, Basic no SSN

TOTAL	1,648
GRAND TOTAL	17,666*

* 6 women unaccounted for

EXCERPTS FROM LETTERS HOME

1943

Dear Friends,

Your letter arrived, today. There is lots of work here, for everyone. This is a "real war zone." Nothing but work. You try to get the gas. We know people who got it come for work here. We will see you, soon.

> Lovingly,
> Mayme Reuber

Dear Sis and Vince,

We got here last night. We rented a cabin and cleaned up. We then got in touch with Father Hennekes, and he invited us to have dinner with him, this afternoon.

He took us on a tour of Phoenix this morning and we saw many things we had never seen before. We are now resting at his place until about 5 p. m. and then we are going to drive, through the desert, around 200 miles to Yuma, Arizona, right on the California border.

Yesterday morning we went to the Grand Canyon National Park. The scenery is beyond description. We nearly melted coming through the desert to Phoenix. At night it cools off so it is real cool—the skies are cloudless and there was a full moon!!

Phoenix is a beautiful city with mountains, palm trees, etc. On our drive, today, we saw cotton fields, orange, fig, lemon, grapefruit trees and had our picture taken in front of a banana tree, by the Capitol. More later.

> Love,
> Niece

Dearest Mother and All,

We're now settled in Mayme's four room apartment, over their garage. It is cute and cool and will have to do as you have no idea how scarce rooms, and apartments, are People want them, so badly, that they just cry when they can't get one, they say. So, even if ours is small, we're very lucky to have a place, at all.

This last Sunday Mayme took a picnic dinner and she, Hank, and us, went over to L. A. and got Clare and we had a delicious picnic dinner. Then we drove about a hundred miles, all over L. A .We saw all the airplane plants—Douglas, Vultee, Vega, Lockheed, etc. You can't imagine the way they're camouflaged! All important buildings, plane runways, bridges, etc. are painted to camouflage them. We also saw all the big shipbuilding outfits. They're astounding! In fact I don't know what we didn't see.

We were to just one dance, so far—last Saturday night. We had lots of fun.

L. A. is such a large city; it is enough to scare the wits out of anyone. The street cars, buses, etc. are so crowded, it's pathetic. Long Beach is so nice and calm along side of L. A. We surely like Long Beach. The weather is cool and the nights are even chilly. There always seems to be a cool, moist breeze. Every day is the same—bright and sunny with few, to no clouds. Would love to have a little home out here, some day. Maybe we will with the help of God—who knows?

Much love,
Seglo

Dear Mother and All,

We had our first day of work, as typists, at California Shipbuilding Corporation. It was really an experience going to work this morning. We went about nine blocks from our apartment to catch a train (really made up of five, red street cars hooked together) and called the "Calship Special." It took us out to Terminal Island, about l2 miles from Long Beach. Our cars leave at four minutes after seven and we begin work at 8 a. m. Dad took a street car to his work, also on Terminal Island.

You should see what happens when the whistle blows and the "graveyard shift" starts running for the "time shacks" and the turnstiles to leave the shipyard. I'm telling you the truth when I say such a sight is too astounding for words. The new day employees (about 175 of us) had to wait until the day shift went on. It was certainly true when Doc said that all you see, for miles, are swarms of people, on crutches, canes, healthy, black, red, white, clean, dirty, fat, skinny, old, medium, young, happy, tired and what have you. Altogether Calship employs around 43,000 and is the largest and fastest yard in the WORLD. They are proud of that record and are working teeth and toe nails to go faster yet.

I feel that the education I received, in just this one day of being in that mob, was really something I'll always remember. No one can begin to describe it to anyone else

We like our little apartment better all the time. It is beginning to seem a little more like home. We do our own cooking and have been having good meals. Our little Frigidaire has lots of goodies. Ha.

Tell Janyce that we'll have to look for something "nice" as soon as we get paid. Ha.

> Love from all,
> Niece

Dearest Mother and Biggie,

Last night Mayme gave us some barracuda fish for our dinner. She even started frying them, for us, as we started our other supper. Tonight she gave us a big dish of macaroni, she had prepared. We are plenty tired when we come home from work but we always get a real good supper.

Last night Niece and I went out to a market quite a ways north of here and did a lot of grocery shopping. Everything is as high, or higher, than at home. Tonight, after supper, we fixed hair, and then Niece ironed and I sewed a few things that needed fixing. There is always lots to do when you work long hours. We leave the apartment at 6:45 a. m. and get home at 5:45 p.m., at the earliest.

We work from 8 to 4:30 with 1/2 hr. for lunch, but it takes the rest of the time getting there, and back, in the streetcar. We all plan on going to San Diego, on Sunday. Would surely love it if you, and Biggie, could be here, too. More later. Dead tired.

Love,
"L"

Dearest Mother, Biggie and Vinces.

We got a letter from Mom tonight and also the suits. Thanks! We got a couple other letters; it is surely fun reading them.

We are working every day. Our Supervisor arranged it so Niece and I have the same day off. This week it was yesterday, (Sunday), so we planned a little excursion. We invited Clare to go with us, and so the three of us, plus Clare, went to San Diego, the Mission at San Juan Capistrano, and Tijuana, Mexico. We wanted Mayme to go, too, but she found out late Saturday that she would be having company Sunday, hence she couldn't go.

Clare came down to our place on Saturday evening. We went to the Municipal Auditorium and heard Ted Lewis, and his orchestra, and saw his floor show. It was very good.

We got up at 5 o'clock Sunday morning and went to 6 o'clock Mass, ate when we came home, and left here about 7:45. The drive was very, very beautiful, right along the ocean, all the way. We drove around San Diego, and ate dinner there. We saw some of the huge airplane factories and saw lots of immense planes flying around and coming in for a landing. They really are "honeys." Then we drove on, 16 1/2 miles south of San Diego, to Tijuana. We had quite a time getting across the border.

First of all there were many cars lined up waiting inspection. Well, they searched the car, asked where we were born, had to show some identification, and get all our money changed into Mexican money before crossing the border.

(You didn't lose a cent in the transaction, as they would change it back to our money as soon as you crossed the border, coming back into the U.S.) The point is their money is of lower standards and Americans would profit too much, by it, in Mexico.

Tijuana is just a little town—all gift shops and trinkets, and people begging you to buy stuff. We stayed until around five and then started home. We had lunch when we got home, about 9:45, and then Niece and I took Clare to the P.E. (Pacific Electric) station, and she went home to L.A. We certainly had a big, and enjoyable, day.

We visited at the Capistrano Mission quite a while. It is simply beautiful—you never saw such beautiful yards, and flowers, in all your life! We got there for part of the 9 o'clock Mass, too. We took some pictures there. I hope they're good. There are many pigeons there and they are so tame they light on your hand, shoulders and head. We had fun with them.

We certainly are busy out here. We get up at 5;15 every morning, rush to pack lunches, get breakfast, do dishes, make beds, get ready, walk 8-9 blocks to the street car, which pulls out for Calship at 7:05. Then rush thru hundreds of workers to our Warehouse, punch the time clock, and start work at 8. Work hard until 12. (We have a 15 minute intermission both morning and afternoon.) We have 1/2 hr. for lunch, then work until 4:30. When the whistle blows, you grab your time card, and then run like the very dickens to get in line to clock out. Then you REALLY run, several blocks, to catch the "Calship Special", crowd into the car—ride to Pine and Ocean St., get off, walk home 8-9 blocks, (tired as a dog), hurry to get into the grocery store before 6, get a big supper and we really do,(every night) because we are all hungry. Then after supper hurry to do dishes, wash and iron sometimes, write letters, press clothes, take a bath, and hurry to bed so we can get up at 5;15, again. Now that is life in California, but we LIKE it!! We have a little fun once in awhile, too.

We had to join the Union at $26 dollars each. That will really make a "cavity" in our checks this week.

After you've all read this, please send it on to Doc.

Am enclosing $10. Tell Janyce to write Aunties. It "behooves" her. Ha.

Much love,
"L"

Dearest Mother, Biggie and Seglo,

How's everything back in good old Minnesota? We are O. K. We received your letter tonight, Mother, and really read it through and through. Well, has Seglo arrived yet? It just doesn't seem possible to think that 2000 miles are between us and home. I guess we are just unconscious or something, but we just can't make ourselves believe it!! We certainly do miss Seglo, but we will have to make up our minds that that is that. We will be very anxious (exceedingly so) to hear of all developments on the home front. Don't delay in informing us immediately as soon as any plans have been formed.

We surely thought and thought about Seglo and her little family all the time, during the days that she was driving home. Surely hope she didn't have any trouble.

Mayme has been getting our groceries for us in the morning when she goes over to the Safeway. That really helps. I almost always have supper ready when Dad comes home, so we eat right away and then he wipes the dishes, for me, and we usually are all done, by seven. Tonight for supper we had boiled potatoes, liver smothered in onions, gravy, bread, jam, butter, tea, and I made butterscotch pudding. We feasted.

Well, people, my eyes are so heavy that I cannot keep them open for five minutes more. It is now exactly nine o'clock. Goodnight, and love by the score, and even more.

> Love,
> Dad and Seglo

Am enclosing a "V."

Dearest Mother and All,

Both of us just got home from work, so while the potatoes boil, and the lamb chops fry, I'll begin my letter to you. We just got through reading your good letter, Mother. You're a brick! You really keep the home fires burning. Wish it wasn't so far so that we could run in for a visit, often. We surely miss you, and everyone at home, but we manage to get along—thank God. We are both well and working every day. Dad enjoys the radio, a lot. At present we are listening to Major Bowes.

Well, Seglo, when are you coming out? I am exceedingly anxious to join the Marines. Which one of the Services did you decide on? Last Thursday (my day off) I buzzed up to the 4th floor of the Pacific Building here, and interviewed the Spars! They sound very good. We would go to Daytona Beach, Florida. They have "darling uniforms." But wait until you hear what I did THIS week, on my day off!!!

Yesterday (Wed.) my day off, I perked to the 2nd floor of the Post Office to Room 207 and interviewed the *MARINES. THEY* have what it takes! I will send some pamphlets! We will go to New River, No. Carolina for our Basic Training. Officers are picked from natural born leaders, after you've been in 4 months. The pamphlets will explain about the uniforms! Did that girl, that interviewed me, ever look "*SNAZZY*" and was she nice.!! I get so *ENTHUSED* and feel so "*YELLOW*" in civilian clothes, that I can scarcely wait until you get out here and we get sworn in. That will all take place in L.A.

You have just their physical—no preliminary one. They said any girl in sound health can pass. The trouble is—after you're sworn in, your papers are sent to Washington, D. C. and it takes around 6 weeks until your Active Duty Orders come. What do you think about that? I asked if you could be sworn in there, and me here, and if we could be kept together. They said that was not possible as you would be from a different district.

Come out as *QUICKLY* as you can and bring Mother with you, for a visit. Be sure!! She and Dad can both be here when we're sworn in. Wouldn't that be thrilling?? I just can't think of *ANOTHER* thing. I just can't *WAIT*. I sincerely feel we've completely WASTED a year and a half. Get here as soon as possible. They already call me "Leatherneck" and "the Fighting Irish Marine" out at work.

Just heard the Marine's Hymn from the Quantico, VA Marine's Barracks at the close of Major Bowes program.

Last Thursday Bea and I went to the Majestic. I met the darlingest *MARINE*. He was too cute for words and a perfect model in his uniform. He had well groomed nails, black eyes and hair, and fair skin. He is in on a ship that is being repaired. He had crossed the Equator 10 times in the last 6 months. He was with the ones that were in Casablanca. We danced all evening; he brought me home and made a date for the next night.

He came and we went to the "Chatterbox" for a while, and then to the Hilton Sky room. Did we ever have an enjoyable time!! We had a darling little table right by the west window that looked down on all the lights in the city. I really felt all right gazing at him!! We were in the room with the Orchestra. We danced, danced, and danced. He was *TOPS* for looks and form, so far, but Callaway still is the best dancer. I had a letter from Callaway the other day.

I also had a card from Bob Weisbrodt; he was home on furlough. Ralph Bradley came over Tuesday night.

Now, Seglo, write *IMMEDIATELY* and let me know what you plan on doing. Bring Mother with you, for a visit.

Be good, everybody. Write. "Happy Birthday, Mother." We love you and wish you many more wonderful birthdays. Hope the package arrived O. K. and that you like the contents.

Love,

Dad and Seglo

Dear Folks,

I just got your letter, Seglo, and read it to Mayme. I certainly do not envy you the stormy weather. I simply can't believe that Minnesota weather is like that when it is so nice, in California.

I suppose you have my letter, by now, stating my preference to join the Marines. I would love to say that I was a member of the Marine Corps—but training with the Spars in good, old, warm, balmy Florida, on Daytona Beach, doesn't sound too bad either, does it?

North Carolina is pretty cold and rainy, I'm afraid—although I'd *LOVE* to be a Marine. What's your decision? Maybe we would be admitted sooner into the Waves, or Spars, than the Marines. You see they have all new barracks, and everything, at New River, for the Marines, and they can only accommodate so many at one time—therefore it would be six weeks or so before active duty call from Washington. What would we do in the meantime? I would hate to leave a $1.03 an hr. job to sit around for six weeks. What do you think is best? Think it over, seriously, and let me know your decision, at once. I am most anxious to join. I think it will be a most valuable experience, and something we will never have an opportunity to do again, in our lifetime.

Lots of "Calshippers" wish me to greet you, for them, Seglo. You say "Greetings" to all the friends, for me.

Be good. Write.

Love to all,
Seglo

Dearest Mother Machree,

How's the little lady tonight? We're just fine and hope everyone, at home, is the same.

We just got home from the market. We went right after supper. Dad did the dishes. He also did them Saturday night, while we got ready to go out. He's a grand sport.

We went to the dance last Saturday night, and had lots of fun dancing with the Service fellows. One in particular. He was a tall, dark, handsome sailor from San Diego. Of all the people I have ever danced with he was the most perfect. He's just darling! He brought me home and made a date for the next night. He came and we went to a nice nightclub named, the "Bombshell" and danced and danced. I could have danced with him much longer, but he had to catch the 12:30 bus, back to San Diego, so that was that. He plans on coming up soon, again. Even Dad remarked about how nice looking he was. Ha. It was a lot of fun.

Love to all,
Bee

Dearest Mother, Biggie, and the Brennans,

How are all of you at home? We are fine and busy as a swarm of bees. We all like the work that we are doing, just fine, and are understanding it better all the time. Dad attended a class in the San Pedro High School, for three days. He gets home, from work, about the same time we do, twenty to six, or so. He enjoys listening to the radio.

Sunday he plans to go down on the Pike for a little while. Usually there are people by the thousands down there. We told Dad if he didn't go down sometime, soon, he'd be going back, to Minnesota, without ever seeing the ocean. Ha. The whole shoreline is a blaze of color with all the beach umbrellas.

Last Sunday we had to work but the crowd was still there, at least some of it was, when we came home from work. It was terrific!!

Last night Mayme went with us to a Market. While we were lined up, waiting our turn to get to the register, a girl smiled and spoke, clear across the store, to us. We did not recognize her until finally we got quite close, and she said, "Didn't you two go to Beauty School in Omaha?" Here she was a girl who went there at the same time we did. She said she might not have recognized us if she met one, alone, but when the two of us were together, she recognized us, at once. She has lived here for two and a half years, and at present is working out at Douglas, as a lead woman, in a metal department. She gave us her address and invited us to come visit her, sometime.

Tonight, L, and I, bought ourselves some new bathing suits. They have a cute flared skirt over them and aren't as short as most of them. We have terry cloth coats that match them. L's is red and white striped, and mine has blue stripes. We purchased them in a shop, down on the Pike. They are cute, and different. We're going to tell Clare to bring her bathing suit down Sunday, and we may get our big toes wet, down in the ocean. Don't worry; we won't be going out, too far.

Goodnight—sweet dreams and be good.

Love to all,

Dad, Num, and Niece

Dear Folks,

Saturday I went down to the Post Office, for some stamps, and while there went up to the Marine Office, on the Second Floor. There was one male Marine in there and three Women Marines. I asked them if they had any idea when we would be getting our call, and they said they thought around the end of January. This one girl was telling me all about our camp, at New River. It is only 8 miles from the Atlantic Ocean. She said it is the prettiest camp that you have ever seen.

She said life in the barracks is one thing that we will never forget. It is so interesting meeting girls, from all over the U. S., and from all walks of life.

The other night Niece and I bought our regulation Marine shoes that we must have. They are a brown, laced oxford, with 1 1/2 in. heel, arch supports and most every thing imaginable. I also ordered the woven name tags that we must have to label all our articles of clothing, (gear, the Marines call it). These tags must be sewn on everything we own, in camp.

Calship launched the U.S.S. Carole Lombard, Saturday, and the yard was all excited over the celebrities present. Niece had a real good close look at Clark Gable, who is now a Captain, in the Army. He was Carole's husband when she got killed, in that airplane crash, a year ago, when coming back to Hollywood., after a big Bond drive. Niece also saw Robert Montgomery, a Lt. Commander in the Navy, Cecile B. DeMille and a couple others that I can't recall right now.

Well, I must close, for this time, and get this in the mailbox. Give this letter to Sis and Vince to read, and give the kiddies a big hug and kiss from their "Auntie Marines."

Much love to all,

Seglo 1. "L"

Long Beach, Calif.
Tuesday night

Dearest Mother and Biggie,

Well, this was Niece's, and my day off, and a very busy one for us. To begin with, we got up at 5; 30, got Dad's breakfast, packed his lunch and got him off to work. Then we went to St. Anthony's church, for what we figured would be the seven o'clock Mass. We got in on the end of the 6 o'clock mass, and the next one was at eight. So we stayed, and prayed, and went to Confession, and then to Holy Communion at the 8 o'clock Mass. We came home, ate breakfast, sat and talked for a while, and then we had some business to do downtown, which took awhile.

There was a big crowd downtown as there was some sort of Army parade, advertising some kind of an Army show that is soon to be here. When we came home we really got busy. Niece tore into cleaning the house, scrubbing, waxing and moving the furniture, washing the window sills, etc. I tore into a wash and hung it up on the roof.

As soon as Dad came home we had supper ready, and we ate right away. Then I did the dishes, scrubbed and waxed the kitchen, and hung up some cute, clean kitchen curtains that Mayme brought up to us. Dad is now listening to a ball game over the radio. Niece is ironing some of the stuff for tomorrow and I said that I would write a letter, home. O, yes, I forgot to tell you that we also fixed our hair in between times, today. We didn't have a minute, even to sit down to rest, but our house surely looks cute tonight, as a result.

This summer has gone on the wings of the wind!! I simply can't imagine that here it is after the middle of August! I surely get the "Blues" when I think of having to leave here. If there were only apartments, of any size, available, I would come back, finish up my business, in short order. Then Mother, you, Biggie and I would hit immediately for the West, for the duration, anyhow. I don't know how I can ever endure that sleepy, dead town after living in the "Paradise of the West." No kidding that is just what Long Beach is. It surely rates tops, with me! Now and ever afterwards! By hook or by crook, I'm finding a way out of my business back there in short order. So I can't say just when we will hit the trail, but it will be before long, so the calendar says.

We had a lot of fun Saturday night. Two nice Army Air Corps Cadets, from Santa Ana, came and they were all dolled up in their best dress uniforms. We went down on Ocean Street, and then we decided to take a boat ride. These are little boats (either single, or double) that you can rent, and ride around in the lagoon, inside Rainbow Pier. The Cadet Niece was with, was from Nebraska, and mine was from the state of Washington. His Dad owns a salmon cannery and my friend was educated in a Military Academy. He went 2 1/2 years to the University of Washington. They were very nice and we had a lot of fun.

Much love from all,
"L"

HI!

"L" forgot to tell that my Sailor friend, the handsome, wonderful dancer from San Diego, came up last Friday night, and we went to the Palladium, in Hollywood, to hear Jimmy Dorsey. Did we ever have fun dancing to such a wonderful Band!!! Tell Doc he hasn't heard anything yet until he hears Jimmy Dorsey.

The Palladium is a grand dance hall in the heart of Hollywood. He went back on the 3 o'clock bus to San Diego. One hundred miles, for a date, isn't bad, eh? It would really be big stuff back there, wouldn't it? Ha.

Love, Mick

At a Los Angeles Station
Saturday—12:30 (Noon)

Dearest Mother, and All,

Excuse the writing as I am using my purse to write on as I am sitting here waiting for the garage man to change the oil and grease the car. We didn't get started quite as soon as we figured due to "gas complications." Now, however, we are ready to hit the trail in a couple hours, or so. Clare is coming with me and a rider to Salt Lake City and one to Boulder, Colorado. Both of them are teachers.

I can't say just when to expect me, so don't worry because we will drive carefully and take every precaution.

Well, I must rush along now and get started. We plan to go to Las Vegas, Salt Lake City, Boulder, Denver, Lincoln, Omaha and home.

I will be seeing you shortly, (with the help of God.)

With love,
Eleanor

Dearest Mother, Biggie and Seglo,

How time flies! Dad and I just finished saying the Rosary. He took a bath, and shaved, while I cleaned the house. We are getting along, but really miss you; Seglo Mayme does most all of our shopping, for us. All I have to do is make out a list, of the things that I want her to get, for us, and early in the morning she goes over to the store, and picks out the best, of whatever we want, and then Carl comes over and takes the stuff home, in his wheel-chair. She puts the meat, or fish, or things like that, right in our refrigerator, so then all I have to do is pay her, and cook the meal. It surely saves me a lot of work, and I sincerely appreciate it. She is TOPS!

How's the new birthday dolly? Wish we could see Jerry walk. We think of the kiddies, so often.

Write often—long letters.

Love to all,
Dad and Niece

Dearest Seglo,

We received your long letter, last Saturday, and certainly was glad to get it, as you well know. I meant to write to you, immediately, but something always presents itself and I don't get around to it. Well, here goes, now.

To begin with, "Happy Birthday, Seglo". Better late, than never. Hope you had a very wonderful birthday. I am sending you a little box and I hope you like the contents. I didn't get down town in time to have it there on your birthday, but I think you will like it just as well anyway, even if it is a few days late. Right?

Everything, out at Calship, is much the same. For some reason, or other, I have still not seen any of my big money. I questioned Tommy about it, again today, and he said that my raise, and several that occurred at the same time, were held up on account of some new form in regard to raises. I told him that I better get it pretty soon or I would be in my grave and never get to enjoy it. Have I been working!

My day off was changed. I had Monday this past week and now I will have this Sunday off and then for another of those beloved ten day stretches. I just got off of one a few weeks ago, but I soon will be on one, again. Yesterday when I was off I got a new typist. Today I got another, so altogether now I have five typists. You might say that all of them are new.

This morning, when I got to work, there was a desk full of proof reading, two new girls to break in, and two boxes full of forms to be written!! We are about as rushed now as we were when we first entered the yard. Remember?

This next Tuesday, (a week from tonight), the Navy is sponsoring a dance for the Calship girls at the Receiving Station, on Terminal Island. "Bee' is going to come home with me, from work, that night and we are going to go to it. Marion and Betty are going, too. Transportation is furnished, and everything, you know. I think it will be fun. Wish you were here to go with us. I really do miss you and think of you, SO often. It is just a big daze, and everything seems so unreal when I think where I really am, and how far from home we really are. But I guess we really asked for it, and now we'll have to make the best of it.

What have you decided to do? After all, it is you that has to live your life and so do just exactly what you think is best.

Tonight Mrs. Williams, from across the street, was over. She said her husband was out at the Roosevelt Base, attending the Bob Hope show. Bob Hope was there, in person, from seven to eight. Maybe, by chance, you heard the program.

Tell everyone "hello."

Goodnight and sweet dreams, darling. Hope you like your birthday present.

Love to all the dear ones, on the Home Front,
From the Long Beach Division of the Herron Defense Workers.

Seglo

Dearest Kids and Kiddies,

Today we received our preliminary orders telling us to stand by, for our formal orders, to leave on February 18th, three weeks from today. These orders were from L. A.—our formal orders will come from Washington, I presume. We are all excited!! We will all convene on February 18th, between twelve and two, at the L. A. Procurement Office, where we were sworn in.

The day before Doc came to visit, I took off from work, and we went shopping and got most of the things we needed, for New River. Everything we bought is exactly alike, only our robes. They are made alike but L's is white, lined in Chinese red, and mine is Chinese red, lined in blue. They are quilted taffeta and have very pretty buttons. They are soft as down. We also got new white slips, and very pretty pajamas.

Our playsuits are blue trimmed with dainty red and white tatting. They have skirts, too. We still have to buy brown gloves, play shoes, and bedroom slippers. I think that will take care of what we need to take.

We had a lot of fun while Doc and his friend, Frances, were here. She seems like a lovely person and they are very fond of each other. She is very friendly and we liked her, a lot. She felt she had a very good time, here, too.

Do write, often—we are always so glad to hear from you.

Be good.
Niece

Dearest Folks,

We received Mother's letter Saturday. I just wrote to Doc, and sent it along.

We got our *ACTIVE DUTY ORDERS!* We will be, in L.A., between 12 and 2, p. m., on February 18th. We are *VERY* excited!! We got more instructions about what we will need to take with us and also two shoe certificates, for additional shoes.

We haven't heard, from Doc, since they returned to Richmond. We surely had a good time together and "Eagle's Nest" seemed real lonesome, for awhile, without them.

We went to 8 o'clock Mass and Holy Communion, yesterday. Gladys and Rudy had us out to a very good dinner last night and they also had another Minnesota teacher whom they know, so we could meet her. They are SO good to us.

I go to 8 o'clock Mass and Holy Communion every morning.

We plan to have a couple girls, from the office, in for dinner, tonight, and to stay with us. Hope Biggie's cold is better and that Jerry and Janyce are well. Please hug them all, for us.

Love,
"L"

1944

Tuesday—12:15 (Noon)
Nearing Atlanta, Georgia

Dearest Folks,

Hope all is well at home. We're nearing our destination—only one day left!! We changed our course, somewhat, and didn't go to St. Louis but cut right across Arkansas, to Memphis, and then Birmingham and Atlanta. We play cards, sing, and try to amuse ourselves. We saw sugar cane and cotton fields. Many of the houses have no windows or doors—just holes cut in the side.

The scenery is much prettier here, than in Texas. We are approaching the Appalachian Mts. We are now in the Eastern Time Belt.

Last night a whole lot of us had a song fest, in the Observation Car. One gal has a piano accordion along, and plays pretty well We go to bed about 10 o'clock. Our compartment is just like a small, private hotel room. We are fortunate to have some privacy.

The trip—climate and all has been lovely. Today is cool and cloudy. The soil here is red clay and we see many brick factories. Last night about 4 a.m. "L" woke me up to look out at the huge blast furnaces in Birmingham. That's the "Pittsburgh of the South" and the only place in the world where coking coal, limestone and iron, (the three necessities for smelting steel), are found in abundance.

By the sound of things we start drilling almost the minute we land. They really start in "tough", they say. Pray for us that we'll be good Marines. More later. Write often..

All our love,
Niece

February 23, 1944

Dearest Folks,

We arrived here safe and sound at 7:45 A. M. We got here ahead of schedule because we were routed differently, and didn't go to St. Louis.

We were met at the train by a group of Marines—Lts, Sgts. Cpls, and what have you. Then came the big trucks; they loaded us in and brought us here to the Recruit Depot.

Our Camp here is very, very beautiful. It is right on the river and is just grand. There are 1500 girls training here and do they ever keep you on the jump! We drilled and everything today. You march, strictly G. I., to everything you do.

There is a lovely church here so we got our Blessed Ashes, today. Everything is a pretty light red brick. Chow is very good. It certainly is a brand new experience, but we like it!

We have inspections, drills, classes, etc. and lights out at 10 p. m., so we'll have very little time for writing, during Boot training, but you write us, often.

Niece and I are "Bunkies." I sleep in the "upper deck" and Niece in the "lower." There are 90 of us in this squad room. It is all new and very nice, but they really "bark" at you. Tough—Oh boy!

Well, I must turn in.

Much love,
Pvt. Eleanor

Dearest dears,

Received Mother's very good letter, today, and we were very happy to get it and hear that all is well, at Home. That means everything, to us.

Saturday afternoon, a gal friend, "L" and I, went to L. A., and Hollywood. Through a USO, we obtained a nice room, in a private home. We visited the "Hollywood Canteen" and got Keye Luke's autograph. He was the "helping star" there, Saturday night. He was always the son in the Charlie Chan pictures. We talked with him, a little. He is very nice. Then we went and danced at the

Palladium to "Woody Herman's" orchestra. Was that something!! Oh, what a crowd, but we had lots of fun. Sunday we went to Mass, in L. A. and then to the show.

Yes, indeed, we're watching the Election, like hawks!! We sent in our ballots with big X's, for Roosevelt, of course.

Work is the same—hard, but we love it, and is it VITAL!!

Must roll into the sack. More again, soon. Glad you hear often from Doc, too.

Love to all, from both,
Niece

Dearest Folks at Home,

Well, here I am back again for another chat. How's everything? We're better than ever, although we haven't gained back any of the weight we lost, when we were sick.

Irish is teaching her Gunner's class again, and I am the only one in our office, so I thought I better click off a few words so you could find something in the mailbox.

It is a beautiful, warm, sunny day, here at El Toro. The air from the surrounding mountains is always real cool—sometimes cold—in the mornings, but about noon it warms up, the mountains clear their mist, and we have another nice day. We haven't had any rainy spell now for quite a while, so we are a little worried that the rain may be waiting for the week-end.

We got Sis's good letter, today—the one she wrote up home on the day you heard about our sick spell. Don't worry about us as we are pretty well protected from most everything—the poisoning was an accident and very likely won't happen again in a hundred years. We thought about not telling you anything about it, but the night I wrote it was so stamped on my mind, that I couldn't think, or write, about anything else. As for fire—we have a girl on watch, all night long. Her main responsibility is to watch the lounges and laundries, etc., for fire. We have a fire department right here, on the Base, so all is well—I hope.

Colonel Ruth Cheney Streeter—the head of all the Women Marines, is to be here on the station, today. There is to be a big review this afternoon, at 4 o'clock, but as we have to teach, we won't have to be in it. Then tomorrow morning, at ten o'clock, she is going to talk to all of us, in the Station Theater. I imagine the main jist of her talk will be about overseas duty. The only place they are sending the WR's, so far is Evah, about thirty miles from Pearl Harbor. Several of our girl friends have signed up. The length of time is two years, with no returning, for any reason in the meantime. We tried to talk a few of them out of it, but they took their physicals and are having their interviews, so I guess they will be going. We feel we have plenty to do on this side of the H20. Ha. Right?

We got to see the Bob Hope show the night he was here. We started standing in line about a quarter to five, and finally about six thirty, they opened the doors and we got in—about three-quarters of the way to the back of the hall, but we could see and hear well—and did we ever knock ourselves out laughing. Frances Langford, Vera Vague, Jerry Colonna, and several other stars were in the show. It was really good. It is sponsored by the Pepsodent Toothpaste Company.

Well, I better ring off and get ready to teach my two o'clock class.

Much love to all, and take good care of yourselves.

Much love,
Mick.

Dearest Folks,

Hope everything is O. K. with everyone, at home. We are fine-both gaining back some of the weight we lost when we were sick.

We went to 7 o'clock Mass, confession, and Holy Communion this a.m. There surely is a big crowd, even at that early Mass. It surely is inspiring to see so many young men, and women, receiving Holy Communion.

Our new PX opened last night. We didn't go because there was such a terrific mob. It is a beautiful building, from the outside, and some of the gals, that were there last night, say it's really nice, inside. It has a Beauty Parlor, Auditorium, Game Rooms, Library, Soda Fountain, etc. We are going over when there isn't such a jam.

We've been really studying hard this weekend on our Aerial Gunnery. We surely like it.

We surely have grand chow. For dinner today we had: chicken, sweet potatoes, dressing and gravy, whole kernel corn, beets, lettuce, dark bread, butter, jam and jelly, ice cream, coffee and tea. We should be able to exist. Right? It must cost thousands of dollars just to feed us all everyday.

Must get ready for bed.

Love to all,
Irish

Dearest Folks at Home,

We had our second Typhoid shots, today, and I'm nearly crippled, so this will be just a note. Hope Biggie, and all of you are well.

It rained (poured) all day, today. Last night, for about two hours, we had a severe electrical storm. I thought we'd all be electrocuted, right in our bunks. Ha.

Here's something important! In case we're ever needed home, on any emergency, let our local Red Cross know, at once. It is through the Red Cross, only, that emergency furloughs are allowed.

Loads of love,
Bee

Dearest Folks,

We're certainly busy gals these days. We're on the "go" every minute and have no spare time. It's the busiest life one ever saw, or ever heard about. When we come home, on our first leave, we'll certainly never get everything threshed over as there is so much to tell you.

Today we saw about 1,000 Marine Gals drilling, in formation, behind our Barracks. It was the most thrilling, and beautiful sight, you ever saw! It is certainly going to be a big thrill when we march in our first review!! They have reviews here every Saturday morning before all the Officer's, in the Officer's stand. This is certainly a place one would never be able to imagine, or visualize, without being here a while The grounds, location, scenery and buildings are so pretty, but boy, oh boy, do we get barked at—everybody does.

We have G. I. parties every Friday night. That means a minute, exacting housecleaning. We wash windows, clean blinds, swab the deck, (on hands and knees,) (every morning by a mop), dust, scrub clothes racks, wash out lockers, etc. The party lasts only from 6:15 to 9 p. m. Not bad, eh?

We all had a lecture on Bonds, today. Everyone signed up, for some. We signed up for an $18.75 one every month—for each. We also signed up for $5,000 life insurance, each.

Well, I must shower, pray and get to bed, before "Taps." We'll write, any and every spare minute we get, but always pray for us that we'll get on O. K. and we're always thinking, and praying, for you, too. We hope you'll be proud of us, some day, with the help of God.

Lots of love,
Niece

March 15, 1944

Dearest Folks,

Here I am sitting, on duty, checking gals, in and out. You see, when they leave to go to the laundry, PX, or Post office, they must tell where they are going and also must write the time they are coming back. For each thing it can be only a limited few minutes.

This was supposed to be our "morning off", but with all the extra cleaning duties, there really is "no time off." Niece, and a bunch of others, got to go this morning, however, to see how they do camouflage work.

We were both on Guard Detail last night. Two girls walk together, armed with a Billy club and a whistle around their neck, to call the Corporal of the Guard, if necessary. We were "supernumeraries" (extras) and so we did "Mess Guard." We stood at the door of the Mess Hall, armed with our "billy club" while all the WR's (Women Reserves) and Officers, filed in to chow. Of course we had to salute all the officers. It was fun. Then we had to sleep in the Guard House, in case any extra guards were needed We didn't happen to be called.

Niece, and four other girls, from our Squad Room of 90 girls, was chosen to go to the Higgin's Boat Landing, tomorrow, to have pictures taken of the famous Marine Higgin's boats. These are the ones in which the Marines make most all of their landings. Niece is real excited. All the kids are wild about the Higgin's Boats. We are all supposed to get a ride in them before we leave Boot Camp.

> Must close.
> Love,
> "L" Write.

Dearest Folks,

I have about ten minutes before "lights out." Yesterday twenty of us girls, a Captain, and a photographer, from the "Look" magazine, were around the camp all day taking pictures, for "Look." In the morning we went about fifteen minutes, in a Marine bus, to a place called "Courthouse Landing", and there we got into a huge Higgin's boat and went all over the bay taking pictures, and then out into the Atlantic Ocean. We made a beachhead landing and had to run out of the boat, like the men Marines.

In the afternoon we took pictures down by the river, here. We all had hold of hands and ran through a smoke screen, etc. The photographer did not know, for sure, when the pictures will come out in the magazine, but be on the lookout.

Tomorrow the class ahead of us graduates and we become Senior Boots. Two weeks from tomorrow we're to graduate. Imagine that!!!

Dearest Folks,

I just got back from our scrubbing detail, so will endeavor to write a line. I hope all of you are well.

Tomorrow afternoon we are to observe a special Weapons demonstration. The male Marines are to fire all the different types of guns, for us. It should be interesting; I hope the weather cooperates. We also started studying about Chemical Warfare and Gas masks, and weapons, today. Each of us was issued a gas mask to keep for two weeks, just to familiarize ourselves, with it. Next week we will put on our masks and go through a gas chamber. We'll really be Marines in every sense of the word, soon.

They have just completed an "obstacle course", for the women. We are to go over it some day this week. It consists of bars, barrels, and I don't know what all. It's really pretty rugged, I guess—but rather fun.

We are to finish here, Saturday, April 1st. That night we are to have a graduation dance—men and everything!! We girls all realize, now, what the boys feel like when they haven't seen, or been with girls, for a long time. We feel the same way!

All of us are getting extremely excited to see what our orders will be!!! We should have been in here exactly a year sooner. All the officer places are more than full and they are closing all the schools. They are planning on stopping recruiting in May, or June, as the quota is already full. Our maximum quota for W. R's is 18,000 enlisted, and 1,000 officers. They have stopped giving Pfc ratings to Boots. You have to go into the field and prove yourself before you get anything, and then promotions will be plenty slow but it can't be helped now. We just will have to pray, and work hard, and God will give us what we deserve.

                 More soon.
                     Love,
                     Niece

Dearest Folks,

We are just back from chow, about half an hour, and have a little time out to write.

Saturday night brings a little rest with it so it is a real breathing spell. Here was our today's schedule. We "hit the deck" at 5:45, of course, as usual, did out details; making our bunks *just* so, sweeping, swabbing and dusting the areas of our bunks, etc., for a very strict G.I. inspection. Oh, yes, last night we had another G. I. party which consisted of *SCOURING* everything—everywhere—so you can easily see there is never any dirt, anywhere, but you have to rub and scrub like you were cleaning a very dirty house.

Then, getting back to this morning, we had to get ready, *JUST SO* and in about ten minutes, and muster for chow. We march, in a certain formation, wherever we go. Had about ten minutes to eat, after standing in the chow line for about 20 to 25 minutes. Rush back to the barracks, for two minutes to get notebooks, etc. Then away we went to the Parade ground, along with hundreds of others, to practice for our first Review, which was just before dinner.

Men GI's drill us, out on the Drill field, and do they ever make us move!! It's fun, though. We have always loved anything military—well we're surely getting it here. Ha. Then after drill, away we rushed to two classes, then rushed back and out on the Drill Field for our very first Parade past the Reviewing stand, and we, your Marines, in full uniform, strutting our stuff, while our all Women Marine Band snappily played the "Marine's Hymn" and other marches.

All the dignitaries of the Post, plus Senator Walsh, were in the Reviewing stand. He is the one who is against the Marines, and Waves, going overseas; so we were especially trying to impress him! Scuttlebutt, (rumor), is that Congress may act on that measure, soon. Some of the gals are wild to go abroad. From all accounts, our Parade was very impressive and our Battalion was complimented.

We were almost thrilled, to tears, as we snappily and smartly, marched along. We have one of those Reviews every Saturday, from now on. Then after the Review we had to rush to our Barracks to stand by our bunks, "at attention", rigidly frozen in place—while everything was really inspected, by a group of about 6-8 big shots. Then we had to stand a personal inspection, after that. It was then chow time. We have very good food.

Then after chow, we dashed to a classroom and spent the whole afternoon writing tests. Back to our barracks a couple minutes, and Niece and I checked out and went to church, where Holy Communion is distributed, every day, at 5 p. m. Then back we dashed and marched to chow, and now I am writing to you. Rather a busy day, eh?

The time is going faster, and faster, now. We surely like it—especially now that we are in full Marine uniform .O, yes, yesterday we got paid—$30 a piece. They pay twice a month and our first amount was $30. Soon they will start taking out our bonds and insurance.

This part of North Carolina is just like a jungle, in the summer. That's why they train men Marines here, for jungle warfare. There are lots of them training on this post—but in a different area—so we never see them in our area, at all. They are strictly forbidden to enter our area!!

We think of home, often, but are well, contented and happy, so don't worry about us.

Give our love to all,
B & L.

Monday night

Dearest Folks, Doc and Vinces,

Hope we are not on the "black list" for not having written sooner, but we have been exceptionally busy, and tired, having just completed Mess Duty. Thank Heavens our mess duty ended last Saturday. Some girls had to do dishes, pots, pans, etc., too. We worked from 5 a. m. until 6:15 p. m. with about 25 minutes off in the afternoon.

Now while we're waiting for our school to open, we're Desk Watcher's, again. We are together, in the office of Bks. 224, from midnight, to 6 a. m. We answer the phone, make sure all doors are secure, check the lounges, and laundries, every hour, for fire, and take care of the wake-up list. We have to go around and call certain ones, at certain times, so they can get to their work. However the entire time, up to midnight, is our own.

The weather is warm here, now, and we are in our summer uniforms. It has been warm and windy all day. At present it is lightning and very likely will rain, soon.

Today we had to attend a two hour class in Chemical Warfare. It was all about poisonous gases, and gas masks. Then we had to put on our gas masks and go through a gas chamber. Just before we left the chamber we had to remove our masks and get one good whiff of it—full blast. Boy, oh, boy, did our faces ever burn, and our eyes smart, and water, for about 20 minutes, and then we had one of the mildest gases that there is. It just proves what harm could, and would be done, to civilians, if gas should ever be used!!

We have a free movie here, every night. We go to some of them. Well, I am dead tired, so will close for now. We will write very soon, again.

Love to all,
Niece

April 3, 1944
10 to 3
Monday

Dearest Folks,

Today is very rainy, and all is astir with excitement, as most all of the big drafts, of girls, are leaving today at some time, or other, for all the various places—Washington, D.C., Quantico, California, Oklahoma, Omaha (Radio Mechanics), and other places. Our big draft of gals leaves for Cherry Point, tomorrow, at noon,

We had several Masses said, in thanksgiving, and also that we will always be kept together. We are very anxious to find out what type work we'll be getting into. Lots say that all that go to Cherry Point, for reclassification, get into Aviation, and usually into what they originally signed up for. Maybe we'll be Control Tower Operators, or something. They mentioned Aviation Instructors, once; we just will have to pray.

A big gang of girls just pulled out for these other places. Such yelling of Orders, and mustering, and excitement, you never did see!

Saturday night we went to our dance that was given by the Quartermaster Corps. About 500 couples, of Marine girls and men, were a real sight to behold. Did we ever have fun! Every girl had a date for Sunday afternoon, but we were only out from 2-4, and then in the evening from 6-9: 30. They certainly are watchful of us while we're under their care.

Everyone is so excited here with all the coming and going, packing, etc. that I can't think of any news. We can each have one suitcase, plus our "sea bag", when we leave here. Our "sea bags" are big sacks with locks on them. They will be sent on to our destination.

> We'll write, soon, again.
> Love to all,
> Niece

Dearest Folks,

Hope everything is fine at home. We are well, happy, and very busy.

This last week, on two different nights, thousands of Marines left, from here, for overseas. We could hear the band playing and from our windows could see them marching to the big Vans that would take them to wherever their ships were located. All the girls were pretty silent as we watched the procession. Chills ran up and down our spines, as that is the closest we will ever come to active combat, to see the men leave. We are all mighty proud to be part of an organization that is playing such a noble and good job, of fighting, for our freedom.

After our schooling we will be instructing Pilots and most likely will be directly release some man for combat. It will be a hard course but, with the help of God, we will manage O. K.

Well, folks, I must close and get ready for chow. Incidentally, I have a date tonight with a French-Italian fellow, from New York City.

Take good care of yourselves, and pray for us.

Much love to all,
Your Marines
Niece

Dearest Folks,

Tomorrow we have our first test in Airplane Identification. In our one week of school we have studied over 20 different kinds of American planes and believe you me we have to really know them. We go into a darkened room, and our instructor flashes them on a screen, at one tenth of a second. At that speed they all look alike. At first it was all a blank, but we did nothing, but study, this entire week end so now we feel lots more intelligent. Thank Heave We also have had to learn the nomenclature of all parts of the 50 caliber Browning Automatic Machine gun. There must be 150 parts, at least. You should see us disassemble, and assemble, the machine gun—oh, boy!

We have another course about tracing and Turrets. We get into a circular tub affair, and push on some handles that start the electric motors, and watch through a gun sight, and with a little electric circle, of light, we trace around all kinds of crazy lines. You'd be surprised how hard it is to keep the light right on the lines. After awhile we'll get right into regular gun turrets.

The course in Flight Theory is interesting—at least, so far. Some math is involved—hope it doesn't become too complicated. Don't think it will. We still have two phases to our work that we haven't had, as yet. They will come during the last week, or so. Also around the end of the 4th week you find out what phase of it you're going to instruct.

More later.
"L"

Thursday—About 11 Bells in the Morning

Dearest Folks,

Just a line to let you know our whereabouts and that we're fine and in good spirits.

We left Camp Lejeune, Tuesday, at exactly noon, for Cherry Point—about 60 miles from each other. Three big Marine busloads, of about 160 girls, landed here at about three thirty. We were assigned to our "Wing" and have about the same barracks set up, as before, only rules are not quite so rigid. We are here on "General Duty" which might include most anything—Mess duty, Guard duty, etc. The food is excellent, everyone pleasant, and we are well cared for.

We had an Indoctrination talk, yesterday morning, by our Woman Captain, Captain Lynch, and a talk by our Chaplain. He seems wonderful. All afternoon we were being classified as to the job we are to have, for the duration.

All of us that came to Cherry Point are positively in Aviation in some form, or other, for the duration. Both of us are classified as "Technical Synthetic Instructors." We will go to school for six weeks and then will instruct Pilots. It is a brand new course, and they are going to train only 120 girls, for the job. We will study all sorts of hard things—aerial gunnery, stripping guns, aircraft identification, etc.

We like it here very much. It isn't as pretty a place as New River, but it is a very large Marine Air Field and planes, of all descriptions, are overhead all the time. We saw a large detachment of male Marines ship out, last night, for active combat. The band was playing for them. It was very impressive.

Love to all, "L"

Dearest Folks,

Finally our school is opened. We started Tuesday, May 16th. It is a 5 weeks course so you can figure when we'll finish. We go to school from 8 to 4:30, with an hour for lunch. You should see us learning to disassemble a 50 caliber machine gun!! It has 6 major parts, each of which contains about 20 smaller parts. We have to learn all the names, how to take them apart, and then how to put them back together. O, boy!! Besides that we have sighting and range, tracing from gun turrets, theory of flight, and lots of instruments, etc, to learn to use. It's going to be plenty rugged but very interesting.

There are 22 in our class. We have both men, and women instructors. We have a lot of movies about our work, many of which are very secretive, and for military personnel only. Some of them are very interesting.

Much love,
Bee

Early Saturday Morning

Dear Folks,

We are on our Desk Watch and it is quarter to 2 a. m., now. Some of the WR's are busy cleaning the lounge room, and were scrubbing in the office, here, preparatory to a strict inspection in the morning. We had a big cleaning party in our Barracks tonight, right after chow.

We are getting to like it better here at Cherry Point right along. It is a very large base and still growing You should just see, and hear, the airplanes taking off, and landing, all times, day and night.

The last two nights we had good U.S.O. entertainment in the theater part of the P.X. We enjoyed it. You should have seen the Marines flock around there. Bushels of them!!

It is nearly 6 a. m. now and our relief will soon be coming. I was busy answering the phone lots and hence the time flew away on me.

Write, soon.
Love to all,

Dear Folks, Sis, Vince and Doc,

We got back about six, tonight, from another big day. We were at the Artillery Range—firing 30 caliber machine guns, and pistols, for "Movietone." We left about nine this morning. Just our class, of twenty gals, and two Women Lt' went. It was very tiresome, but fun, firing the guns out over the Ocean. I got to be up in a turret, today, and fired about 600-700 shells (at six cents apiece) at a sleeve, towed by a B25 Billy Mitchell plane. You barely touch the trigger and do those guns ever "shoot the works." They really talk!!!

We then went to the Pistol Range and fired at targets. Out of the first ten shells I fired, I hit the bull's eye four times, and hit the target two other times, and missed four. My instructor said it was good, and that lots of fellows did much worse—so that was something. We took our picnic lunch along and ate by the Atlantic Ocean.

School is fine. We started another phase of our training, today, called 3A2 Trainer. You go into a dark room and planes flash on a screen and you have an electrically controlled gun that you fire at the attacking planes, giving them so many ring leads, etc., and the machine records your score.

Cherry Point is the largest of three places where girls are trained for Synthetic Training. Columbia, S. C., and Pendleton, are the others. Our work really consists of bringing actual combat conditions, into a classroom, and instructing how to cope with them . It is the most up to the minute work a girl can do and we love it!!!

104 new girls arrived here, today, from Boot Camp. This is a shipping out point, for gals. They're constantly going, and coming. You meet a lot of nice girls. and then you soon are separated, again.

           Much love,
           Bee

Dearest Folks,

We had a lovely week-end with Rudy and Gladys, in Long Beach. We were fortunate in obtaining a ride into Long Beach, so we decided to go visit our former office friends, at Calship. You should have heard, and seen, how surprised and excited they were to see us!!. We surely hampered production that day. We were all dolled up in our dress whites—they nearly bowled us over with compliments. We had a great afternoon!!

We then rode back into Long Beach with a man and his wife, from the office, and met Rudy and Gladys, and then to the dance down on the Pike. We had a marvelous time.

Sunday morning Rudy took us to 9 o'clock Mass and then they took us to Knott's Berry Farm, for dinner. It's located about 15 miles from Long Beach. We had a wonderful dinner and then spent a couple of hours going over the grounds, and through "Ghost Town", which is a replica of an old frontier town.

             Loads of love to all, from both-
             Niece

Dearest Folks,

It is a lovely morning here, as usual. The planes are roaring outside of our building, warming up, for take off.

I teach the Jap battleships, and a review of our 10 types of American battleships, to our Gunners class this P.M., from 12:15 to 1:15. Bee is teaching in Group 41 this morning (that is across the field where we have been observing.) She is teaching the Jap fighter planes, today. We love our work, and our Lt. in charge is very nice.

             Love,
             "L"

Dearest Folks,

We went into Santa Ana (about 10 miles) last night as we had some of our shoes in there getting fixed. Then we went to the show—Bing Crosby in "Going My Way" It was exceptionally good.

Have to prepare for my classes, so will close for now.

             Much love,
             "L"

             September 14, 1944

Dearest Folks,

Hope you are all well, and happy as are we. We are very busy with our teaching. We instruct between 150-60 Pilots a day, plus 50-55 Gunners so at the end of a day we are rather fatigued. Today is test day for our Pilots. They are all 1st and

2nd Lts. and we have one darling Captain in class. It is a dirty shame we aren't allowed to date Officers. Of course we visit with them in the classroom, and our office, before and after classes and they are really nice. They joke, tease and cut up just like a big bunch of kids. Of course most of them are only in their early twenties.

They are nearly all "Corsair" Pilots and they'll hardly tolerate one nice word to be said about any other plane. Ha.

Love to all,
Niece

Dearest Folks,

This morning we had to carry our mattresses out. Once every four weeks all of them must be carried to a certain place and thrown over some racks, to air. Every Friday is linen change day.

This morning the "Command" (that is all of us) is to be paid at 8:20. We have to line up alphabetically and there being so many of us it takes quite a little while.

A certain % of the Personnel is to get a 5 day leave either over the Christmas or New Year Holidays—which doesn't count against your furlough time. We are putting in for Christmas and are going up to Doc's.

It is time to get going now as we are giving all the Pilots a big test, today.

Lots of love.
Irish

Dear Folks,

One of our Gunner students, that we knew very well and really liked, and his Pilot were killed yesterday, practicing Dive bombing. The Gunner lived in Detroit and was a cute kid about 21-22 years old. They get killed quite often, here. It is so sad.

Love from both,
Mick

November 16, 1944

Dearest Folks,

We have 347 Pilots on our records now, taking Recognition, and Monday I had a class of 30 Radio Gunners begin the course. Their class is from 12:15 to 1:15 every day. The gunners are all enlisted and rank from Corporals up to Master Tech. Sgts, which is as high as an enlisted person can go. They are a very nice group…

Mick is teaching this class now (the 10 o'clock one) and I'm caught up with the records, attendance, etc. so am typing this note off to you.

It is time for us to go to chow right after this class so I can get back for my 12:15 class.

Must rush along now so until tomorrow—

Much love,
"Irish"

Dearest Folks,

Hope you are all "4.0", as are we. Irish went over to Group 41 again today. We are going to take two days apiece. I'll be going, soon, if I don't get my wisdom tooth pulled. I went over to the Dentist this morning, but as they are very busy with the men, who are soon going overseas, I was asked to come back this afternoon when they may not be as busy.

Today is another gorgeous day, so bright, sunny and warm. Hope the weather is behaving back there now. Suppose the farmers are in full swing getting their crops in, again.

Honestly, they better teach Recognition in high-schools or colleges, or even grades, after the war, as that is the only thing I believe I'll ever be interested in. We love it better every day. We read all the material, from Headquarters, that is really only for officers to read. We tell our boys about all that stuff before they've even seen the magazines.

Many of our new fighter planes are now being equipped with rockets. The Rocket school is next door to our room, so in any spare minute, we're reading about rocket installations, on planes, and seeing movies on rockets, etc. Besides that we're always studying about the mechanisms of our planes, propellers, water-injection, carburetors, firepower, etc. One thing leads to another so, all in all, you have a full head. Ha. Everyone marvels at the way we can quote statistics, facts, and knowledge about planes, ships, etc. Some day we may be experts on the subject, who knows? Ha.

Remember, how when we were first contemplating about joining the Service, you used to wonder if we would really like it after we were in for a while? We never have regretted entering, for one moment, and we wouldn't exchange our knowledge, or our experiences, for any amount of money.

Love and the best of wishes to all our dear ones, at Home.

Your Marines,
Mick

Dearest Folks,

We spent last Saturday night, and Sunday, in L.A, with Clare. Through our USO we obtained free tickets to the Coast's outstanding melodrama, "The Drunkard." It's an old fashioned play that has been running for twelve years!! Sunday p. m. was a matinee for only Service kids. Did we ever have fun!! After the play they had different acts, and a song fest, in which we all joined. Tickets usually coast $1.50 and $2.10. Clare had seen it last year and would like to have gone again, but as it was for Service people, only, she couldn't.

After it was over, about 4:30, we went back to her room and then we went and ate at the "Biltmore." Our "dress whites" really bring forth the compliments and exclamations!

Much love,
"L"

Dearest Folks,

Some of our Squadrons, of Fighter Pilots, are breaking up as so many of them are going over seas and a lot of the others are going to Cherry Point for training as Night Fighters. So, for the present, our classes are not as full, as usual. Some of the boys are constantly dropping in to catch up on the latest, or to bid us goodbye. It seems such a shame that they have to go, but those that are going overseas are tickled as that is what they have been constantly training for, and they are tired of waiting.

Well, the day before yesterday, the phone rang and it was the Intelligence Captain from Group 4l, (the group across the field), and he wondered if we had some information we could give him on JMST (Japanese Merchant Shipping Tonnage.) That is secondary in importance only to the Jap Planes. It is considered high priority strafing material.

The Japanese haven't much of a fleet left so they have to depend chiefly on merchant shipping to bring in their much needed supplies from their conquered islands, and possessions. That's where our planes come in to strafe them, shoot their rockets at them, and to bomb them. Of course our Pilots have to know our landing craft from the Jap merchant ships, or the results will be costly.

Well, we told the Captain that we had a lot of material, slides, etc. He seemed so "stressed out" about the whole affair that we volunteered to go over to his Squadron and teach it, for him. Imagine!! It happens that in that Group, many of the Squadrons teach their own recognition to their pilots'. They teach right in the Briefing Room—where the Pilots are given the last important "Word" before taking off on flights, etc. That group has never accepted WR's, very well,—thinking they were incompetent—so we were doubly determined to sneak in there and give them an A-1 "Snow Job"—and believe you me that is exactly what we did!! Was it ever fun!!!

Did we ever put over that lesson! Irish wrote the outline on the board and I taught the lesson. Did they ever sit up and listen and you should have seen the Intelligence officer sit up in the front seat and watch every word as it came out of my mouth. After I had finished he said it was a wonderful job. Consequently, he has us scheduled to go over there tomorrow, at 10, and again at 1 p. m. He simply marveled at our ability to put such stuff across.

We were told this morning that we two know more about Recognition than anyone on the entire Station!!. And that's something!!! We read, and study it constantly, and the more we study the better we love it. I don't know when we'll ever be able to do any kind of a job after such an important one and one that is so looked up to in the Marine Corps. It is certainly God's grace that helps us remember all the stuff we do and to have such a constant and lasting interest in our work.

You may not believe it, but both of us would rather be down at our work than on LIBERTY. We wouldn't dare tell that to anyone—they just simply wouldn't believe it, but it's true. We look forward to going to work every day. So, now while our classes are smaller, over here, we're going to help that Captain every time we can, until our own attendance picks up, again. I just thought I'd give you a sample of the things we're called on to do.

Love and best wishes to the home gang from the Marines. Write.
Mick

Dearest Folks,

We went down to Quartermaster's this morning and bought our new white shoes, for the summer. Irish also bought a pair of white gloves. I have some from last summer that I never even wore. We're getting all set to go up to Doc's, you see.

What do you think about "VE" Day?? Quite a thing, isn't it? Only wished it meant more than it really does. "VJ" Day will be more important, I think. Whatever are we going to do with all the starving people all over the world is beyond me. We'll certainly have to trust in God that all will be well.

Tonight we're having VE services in Father Scullly's office. (He's our Catholic Chaplain.) After they're over, a bunch of us girls are going to stay and have a little farewell party, for him. Mary, a good friend of ours, who works a the Officer's Mess is having one of the baker's, there, bake a cake and then we are all chipping in buying ice cream and we're presenting him with small gifts, and a spiritual bouquet.

It isn't too much of a party, but at least it will show him that we will all miss him. He is a wonderful, quiet type, person. We hope he will write us when he gets overseas.

Love and best wishes to Sis's and all,
Your Leathernecks—
Mick

Dearest Folks,

The reports are starting to come back, from our boys, overseas, that some of them have shot down some "Jap planes." Of course it makes us very happy, but along with good reports also come some sad ones. One of our boys just had shot down a very fast Jap Reconnaissance plane, and was fast on the trail of another, and he was so close to it, that when it blew up, he was killed, too. But that is war!!

Another of our buddies, was killed last week while up at Mojave in training, just before shipping overseas. Something happened and he had to bail out of his plane and his chute never opened. He was a very close buddy to the other Pilot we wrote you about before, that was killed in a mid-air collision, right here over the field, just a couple weeks before Easter. Well, I guess that is enough of gloom.

It is a beautiful day here, today. In fact, we have been having lovely days all the time of late, no fog, or anything. I guess our summer is here, for sure. Hope the weather back home is nice, too, and that things are growing nicely.

I hope you are all well and it won't be long now until you will be seeing Mick, on furlough, and she will give you all the "word", on everything, out here at El Toro, in person. Above all else, take care of yourselves. Remember that allotment is for you to use, and not to be saving it. That is sent for you to use currently, to get all kinds of good things to eat. Now remember that is an order, that is why we are sending it to you wonderful folks. We want you to enjoy it.

Much love to all,
IrishDearest Folks,

Dearest Folks,

The Commanding Officers, of all the Squadrons, are really putting the heat on our Pilots to attend Recognition, so our classes are bigger than ever—that makes it interesting. We must have better than 400 enrolled now.

Last night we went to the 6 o'clock show, "Meet Me in St. Louis." It is very new, and very good.

Much love,
Mick

Dearest Folks,

Everything at work is super-duper. I am teaching two classes of Gunners this week. One is a brand new class. Of course we always have our five classes of Pilots.

They are all swell fellows. I was just talking to one of my ex-Gunners and he said he and his Pilot just made an emergency landing. This kid was still in his flying togs. They have their life in their hands every day it seems. One of our favorite Gunners was killed practicing dive-bombing about 6 weeks ago.

Well, dears, I must get busy so will say—"bye", for now.

Much love to all, from both—
Mick

Dearest Folks,

Well, it was just a year ago today that you two started on your way home from California. Remember? Tomorrow is our anniversary of being in the Corps for the whole sum of a year. It surely has gone fast and never for one instant has either one of us regretted joining. Quite the contrary we love it better every day and that is the sincere truth.

We simply LOVE the Corps!!! I won't be having my two classes of Gunners today, and tomorrow, for they did so well in buying bonds, in the last Bond Drive, that they gave them two days holiday. I'm glad for the gunners for sometimes they aren't treated as well as they should be, it seems. Lots of them have as much as 22 months of service overseas.

When we moved into our new building, you know that was just at the time that Mick and I got out of the Dispensary, and so we were plenty weak. The Gunnery School was being moved into this new Synthetic Building too, and so they weren't having any of their other classes and were available to help in the settling of their rooms. Some of them saw Mick and I, very slow on our pins, and trying to straighten our room and get it settled.

They came in and took the brooms, and mops, from us and said, "You kids aren't able to do this, let us do it for you." Well they stayed and did everything that we wanted them to fix for us, hung pictures on the walls, polished the tables in our room with furniture polish, and everything. Some of the ones in charge of them, in the Gunnery School, said they couldn't understand it; all they had to say was that "Irish" wanted something done and they would even leave a strenuous game of football to come on the run, to do our bidding.

All we do is treat them like human beings, but that is quite unusual in the Marine Corps, or any other military organization, because it seems that most everyone, who has any jurisdiction over anyone else, tries to show their authority.

Mick and I bought a cute little Christmas tree, in Santa Ana, for our classroom, and then when we went to get some decorations for it, they were completely out of the question. You can't even buy one little icicle. Good were the days when you could get them by the score.

A week from tonight, at 4:30, our five day Christmas furlough begins. Gee, we surely are getting excited about going. I know it will be a lot of fun. I hope that the kids will be able to get up Home for awhile, on Christmas, as I know it will seem pretty lonesome, but if all of you, that are back in Minnesota, can be together, and we three that are here in California can be together, that will be the next best to all being together.

We had a letter, from Gladys, yesterday, asking us to come into Long Beach this week end because they had made some plans, that included us, and she needs to know, for sure. Well, we are in the process of making up our minds because a couple of our students, (Lts.), want to meet us in Long Beach this weekend and take us dancing. I still don't know just what we are going to do.

The weather is still grand out here. Doc said that the weather has been nice there too, and he hopes that it doesn't be raining all the time when we are up there, for Christmas. I think that we will be going on the Bus. You just have to go any way that is available.

I better get busy so will close for this time.

Much love to all from both,
Irish

Dearest Folks,

We received your very interesting, and grand letter yesterday, Mother, and were exceedingly glad to get it. I'm sure it must feel great being back home, again, after being sick. Please take good care of yourself; you are the "greatest."

We had a letter from Doc, last night—I'll enclose it-if I don't forget. His letter was short and sweet. Ha. We hope to be able to go up to 'Frisco a week from tonight—the 11th. If we get a 48 hr. pass, and take three days of our furlough, we will leave here Friday night, at 4:30, and come back Wednesday. That will be just a nice, little jaunt. Hope the Big Shots of the Conference don't go home in a huff before we get to see them. Right?

We went to see Bing Crosby in "Going My Way" last night. We had seen it once before. I believe I enjoyed it more this time than the first. See it if it comes around, if possible.

I'll let you in on a little secret. Sometime in early June you better have the kettle on for a cup of tea—because I'm coming home, on furlough. How about that? Will we ever visit! We'll really thresh over everything.

                                        Love to each of you,
                                        Mick

Dearest Folks,

Doc will be planning on our coming but as we won't know, for positive, until about Wednesday. We will send him a wire so he will know just when to expect us. I know that we will have a marvelous time, as we had at Christmas. Wouldn't it be grand to get to see some of the delegates from the foreign countries, just merely for curiosity if nothing else, and when one has such a splendid chance, I think we would be foolish not to go, don't you?

Father Scully is still with us. We have been going to Mass every day, but we missed this noon, because we had to go to the Tailor Shop with our uniforms, etc., and then we had to hurry back to the office.

We are enclosing a little gift for you, Mother, for Mother's Day, and be sure to do something special for yourself, with it, just for ONCE. You have always done things for everyone else, all your life! The money isn't that much, but the sentiment that goes with it, couldn't be more, under any circumstances, my dear. We wish you the happiest Mother's Day to the BEST Mother that anyone could ever have!!! Had all our plans worked out just so, Mick would have been home for your surprise, but she will soon be at any rate, and then she can tell you lots of things, in person, that it is hard to express in writing. Remember, I'm saving my furlough until such time, as we get the word that we have a place for you Folks, and then I will come a spinning home.

So, until later,
The best of everything to all of you,
Much love from "Your Marines"
Irish

Dearest Folks,

Most mornings the sky is quite cloudy but then about 10 o'clock it clears up and the afternoon is nice. One can always bank on the sun shining part of the day, anyway. How's the weather back home?

It sounds so natural to hear that Dad has some of the garden in already. I hope he doesn't plant too much as it takes a lot of work, and time, to care for it. Suppose Sis has a lot of garden it and some of it up, already.

We should be leaving Friday night for San Francisco. It would be something to be able to say in after years that we got to sit in on some of those Peace Meetings, wouldn't it?

Love to all,
Irish

Dearest Folks,

Hope everyone at home is fine. We're both just getting rested a little after our big sojourn to San Francisco. We had a great time and are really glad we went. San Francisco is a beautiful city and a good place to have a lot of fun. We saw many interesting places, and things

We don't plan on going any place this weekend. In fact I don't think we'll be going far for quite a while. Ha. I'll have to save now for my little sojourn home. I believe that I'll be getting off from work—approximately on Friday, June 29th.

That isn't for sure, but around that time. How will that be if I'm home for the 4th of July?

Won't we have a good time? I'm getting so excited, even thinking about it. Our friend, Ruth Goldstein, is leaving, by plane, for New York City, to be married. She's a swell kid!

Hope your cold is much improved, Mother, and that Dad, and Biggie, are well. The end of the first year of school, for Janyce, is certainly approaching fast, isn't it? I still can't imagine her going to school. It seems like she should still be about 2 years old. Jerry must be darling talking so much, now. I can't wait to see them, too. Tell Vince that I'll expect about a dozen gallons of home-made ice-cream and Sis better start scraping the carrots for some of that famous salad I love so much.

I guess I told you that Doc bought me a nice, Elgin wrist-watch while we were up there. You remember mine was lost, or stolen, while at Cherry Point and I haven't had one, since. It's been terribly hard trying to get along without one, teaching, and everything. It is darling. I just love it. I can't believe I have a watch, again. It keeps perfect time. Doc is so darn good hearted and almost embarrasses us as he is so proud of us being Marines. He almost adopts any Marine he sees, he thinks so much of us. It's too bad that he never got into Service, but he has done far more, as a civilian, than lots have that are in the military.

Father Scully is now overseas; he left while we were up in 'Frisco.

> More later. Be good and don't get sick.
> Love from your Marines,
> Mick

Dearest Folks,

This is Monday morning, again. Mick went a across the field to teach, this morning, and I am alone in our office here on this side of the field. The Lt. was just over here for a few minutes, but is gone already. Ruth is in New York, as you know, so that leaves our quarters very quiet.

I got my correspondence course Saturday noon, one that I am taking through the Marine Corps Institute, in Washington. The name of it is "Pacific World". It is all about the islands in the Pacific. It looks like it will be very interesting. Mick is taking a course similar to it, mostly about Japan though, but hers isn't here, yet .Then we are going to take a course, in English, from the United States Armed Forces Institute, which also will count on our college credit, from Mankato. We wrote in there to find out if they would accept these courses, and they said they would. So, besides having something interesting like that to do, we will be getting credit for it. Not a bad idea, is it?

We went into Mayme's this week-end. We had a lovely time, as usual. We went in on the P. E. bus, at 4:25, from Santa Ana, and got into Long Beach about 5:30. We visited, at Mayme's and then a couple of sailors that we had met before, came, and we went dancing, and had a lot of fun.

Sunday we went to Mass, of course, and had a good dinner. We all took naps and we came back on the bus at 6:15. Leaving on that bus always gets us home early and then we get things nicely lined up, for Monday. We got a good rest, and today we feel as chipper as a sparrow.

           Much love to all at Home,
           Irish

Dearest Folks,

Here, at El Toro, in the Marine Corps, it is just another day, but it is a wonderful sunshiny one, and we are in the best of spirits. Mick is getting more and more jubilant all the time, thinking about coming home, on her furlough. Now she can say it is "this month", anyway, so it is that much closer. I know just how she feels, and can hardly refrain from coming, too, but I must keep my time in reserve, and you know for what. A furlough is good, anytime, but when you know someone else is getting all steamed up about it, you can hardly keep from going, too. Such is life around 1500 girls!!

I just read in our Station paper this morning, "the Flight Jacket" that Aviation Base Reserve Group, commonly known around here as ABG-2, will be up here, from North Island, shortly. They have been coming up here since last fall, and haven't arrived yet, are due to arrive before long. This will make many, many, more girls on the Station—just about twice the amount here, so you can see what it is going to be like around here.

The reports are coming back all the time, of our boys out there in the Pacific, shooting down Jap planes, and of course, some of the poor darlin's being killed, too. Bless their hearts!! That is war!!

A couple Lts., just back shortly from overseas, were just in here, and asking about the latest developments on our American planes. Gee, but it is fun to know that stuff cold and be able to give them the "word" on all the dope. We just LOVE our work better every day.

Until the next epistle, be good, and be planning on Mick's visit.

With Oceans of love,
Irish

Dearest Folks,

Today is the 7th already. Won't be long now until I'll be packing my suitcase. I can't make myself believe that it's true. Boy, will that be something! I think I'll appreciate this furlo', at home, even more than my first one, but I don't see how that could be possible.

Does darling Biggie know that I'm coming home? I'll be so happy to see her, again.

News is scarce so will close until tomorrow. See you, soon. Be good.

Love from both,
Mick

Dearest Folks,

This is Saturday and of course we never have classes on Saturday, because we have to have one day, at least, to sort of catch up with our reading, reports, etc. A lot of the boys came this morning,—ones that didn't know we didn't have classes on Saturday

A Lt. was in this morning telling us that starting this Monday, we will be having gobs of Officers in our classes as we will be having another couple of Squadrons. Boy are we glad, but we already are so busy that we scarcely know what to do. We love it that way!! Mick, and I, instructed 319 Pilots this last week, and I'm sure this next week it will be many more. We are training whole Squadrons that will be going aboard a Carrier, together, from the Commanding Officer on down through the whole bunch. The two head ones of the Squadron are Majors. They all have been Overseas, but are getting ready to go, again.

I think we wrote you how we go right over into the Squadron, of 464, and teach both the Pilots, and the Gunners, in the same class. We have more fun, but boy, oh boy, it is all a lot of work, too!! That is what we joined for, and we surely feel fine when we feel we have done a good day's work

The other night we met a Gunner who we used to teach when we first began, almost a year ago. He said he just had a letter from another Gunner,. and he wanted to tell us what that Gunner had said. It was very complimentary toward our class and instruction. We thought he was giving us a "snow job" but he said it was the actual truth and he thought he had the letter back in his locker, and he would show it to us.

Irish just left for chow, so I will finish this. The sum, and substance, of this whole big sentence is that the Gunner overseas wrote that the training we gave him, in Recognition, had the one and only thing that he learned in his Ground Training that was actually come to his assistance now. It makes us feel pretty good when he hear stuff like that. Right?

                                            Much love from your Marines,
                                            Mick

Dearest Folks and Sis's,

How's everyone, and everything, on the Home front, today? We hope you are "first rate", as are we. We're busy as beavers, again. We have our six classes per day here, and then each morning from 0800-0900 we go right into the Squadron of 464 and teach their Pilots and Gunners. So that makes 7 classes for us. That's a pretty busy schedule, together with keeping their attendance records, sending in reports of attendance and marks to their CO's, keeping our classroom and office clean and dusted, etc. It keeps us hopping, but we love it, so that's all that's necessary, isn't it?

ABG-2 (Aviation Base Group 2), from North Island, (San Diego, is just moving up here this week. They've been building hangars and buildings, for months, for them, and finally they're coming up. Reports have had them coming since last

October. One of our friends, that used to be at El Toro, Marge Murphy, is back here, again. She said it was like she was going home. Her brother, Ed, is, at present, stationed at the Army Redistribution Center, at Santa Ana, awaiting discharge from the Army.

He came over to see Marg last night and we met him. He's very nice—a graduate of the College of San Francisco. We went up and watched them bowl for awhile, walked around and showed him our base, and talked. He thinks he'll be going home,to San Francisco, in another week. He was a gunner in a B-24. His mother gave a party for 25, (five crews), of his friends, the night before he left, for overseas. Out of the 25, only five lived through it. Not good, was it?

Today things really started to hum here in earnest; more like the days of yore. I had only 29 officers in my first class this morning and 40 in my second class—mostly 1st Lts., Capt's, and Majors.

Best of everything,
Irish

Dear Folks,

I hope that the weather warms up and stays that way pretty soon back there in Minnesota so things can grow.

We taught 574 men last week. Busy, eh? I shall surely miss Mick when she is home on leave, when I shall have all the classes myself.

Best regards to all,
Irish

Dearest Folks,

How is everyone? I am fine, but as busy as a little peanut merchant. Today Mac Carthy came over and taught the eight o'clock class here in the classroom, while I taught in the Sqd. I had a big bunch over there, as usual.

We have been extremely busy and especially so as that fellow has been here, again, giving those tests for the fellows to get their CAA licenses and they have been busy writing those tests. They are always in, and out of here, getting pens, ink, pencils, etc. You know how they are, Mick. Even Captain Smith hides his plotting board here in our office, so he will have it every day over here, and not have to cart it along with him. He is Ass't. Ground School Officer, now, for his Sqd. And you should hear him laugh at all the work the new job has thrown upon him.

They had a big Regimental Review, today, and boy was it ever hot!! The girls just more than keeled over, they said. We didn't have to go, naturally, because we are so busy.

Much love,
Irish

Dearest Folks,

I taught the first class this morning, and now at the present Mick is in there giving the boys "the word." We saw by this morning's paper that one of our battleships, the Maryland, is in the Los Angeles Harbor. We want to get to see it. They have released the word on the ones in the Harbor now, so we will be able to see more of them.. We hope so, at least! So, probably when Joe and Doc are down here we will be able to go over and see if we can get aboard. We just simply love that stuff!! We feel while we are in uniform we might just as well take some of the opportunities offered us. Right?

More tomorrow; take care of yourselves.

Much love from "Your Marines",
"Irish"

Dearest Folks,

We spent the weekend on the Station and a girl friend, Mick, and I went bowling this afternoon. We had a lot of fun..

We went to 8:30 Mass this morning and to Holy Communion. Our new Chapel is just beginning to take shape. They were long enough in getting around to building it, it seems, but it is going to be very nice.

Did we ever have a wonderful dinner today—roast turkey, dressing, gravy, corn, buttered asparagus, sweet potatoes, cream of tomato soup, a choice of three salads, pickles, apple sauce and ice cream, hot tea and coffee, and then of course, light and dark bread, gobs of butter, jam and jelly, etc.

Mick and I sat across the table from each other and laughed as we looked at our trays of food. Mick said, "There must be something radically wrong with us, when we can't gain wait and eating all that we do." Ha.

I am writing in our upstairs lounge-so guess I will sign off and go in and see what Mick is doing. She's in the Wing.

Until later—

Much love,
"Irish"

Dearest Folks,

Sunday we got up and went to 8:30 Mass and Communion, and then we went to Inglewood—about 45 miles from here—to the Giant Air Show. The Main show started at 2 o'clock. We were fortunate and obtained good seats, in the Grand Stand, where we had excellent visibility.

We're both about ill today from such excitement. I never expect to ever see anything so thrilling, again. All the fastest, newest Army, Navy and Marine planes were in action—and I DO mean ACTION! Flying at speeds of 500 miles an hour, or better, they would fly very low over the field, and grandstand, and we'd almost have to hang on to our hats. Our backs our just stiff, today, from trying to watch the Jet P-80's and the part Jet, Fireballs. It was really a wonderful show and we enjoyed it from beginning, to end. It lasted until about six o'clock The Army performed from two to four, and the Navy from four to six. It was perfectly wonderful!!

Goodbye and God bless you.
Mick

Dearest Folks,

We certainly have some darling, and smart, Officers in our classes. Most of them are lovely but one, or two, would like to be smart alec, but we give them the "Word" and they behave pretty fast. We're their superiors, you know, when they're in your class. It's a shame that we're not supposed to fraternize with them as other fellows seem rather dull and drab, after talking and associating with "bars" all day. Ha.

This week we taught Japanese and American Carriers (CV's) and Carrier Escorts (CVE's, to our boys. It's fascinating, and pertinent information to learn. We gave them a big test today. Guess they all know, by now, that we were teachers before. The different ones said they could tell. Some said it was our voice, others said our manner, our enunciation and pronunciation, and just the way we conducted class. Ha.

It is rumored that "Bob Hope" is to be at our station, soon. Keep on listening and see if you can hear that broadcast. Don't just know when, for sure.

Take good care of yourselves and we'll do the same. Please pray for us.

> Send this on to Doc, too.
>
> Much love to all,
> Mick

Dearest Folks,

Irish is teaching her Gunner's Class now and I just got back from chow. I have just a few minutes so I thought I'd write you a little note.

Today is beautiful and sunny. The lawns around the Ad Bldg., etc. are green and the flowers are blooming. It is hard for us to realize that it is cold, at home. When one is out here it seems like it should be warm, and bright "all over the world." Wish you all could be out here in the sunshine, however, instead of back there in the land of ice and snow. Well, there'll come a day.

Our classes have been very big all morning. It is certainly a grand and glorious feeling to see Captains and Majors walking into your classroom and sitting down and you stand up in front and give them the latest word on all the American and Japanese planes, etc. Of course all the Pilots are required to take it—it was for 20 hrs. and now it is 35 hrs. of Recognition. Quite a few of our higher up officers come back for extra classes even after they have their required number—so a person feels good as they must think it is worthwhile.

This morning we were giving them the word on many of the newest Jap planes. They don't make very many of any certain type and are always introducing some new type, so it takes a regular Philadelphia lawyer to try to keep up with them. However, we are always studying, and it is fun to keep up with them, as best we can.

Right now I can hear Irish in the next room giving the Gunner Boys the word. She is teaching them the Jap Navy. This particular class of Gunners is especially interesting, and do they ever listen when Irish stands up and tells them something. They always call us Mick, and Irish. Don't you think they are cute names? We like them a lot, and that is all we are ever called now.

>Be good. Write.
>
>Much love to all,
>Mick

1946

Dearest Folks,

Today is the first day of work after our lovely furlo'. We did enjoy it so—especially the fact that we were both home together and we feel we accomplished quite a little. Hope you're all fit as fiddles and that none of you feel any worse the wear for our sojourn home. As Irish told you in her letter, we arrived safe and sound, Saturday night in Long Beach, and stayed at Mayme's until last night—Tuesday.

Everything is much the same, at the Station, with the exception that lots more of the girls have gone. Very soon Irish and I will the two, and only interviewers. One of the girls left, today, and Dottie, the other girl, that we thought would be staying until the end, is planning on getting married around the first of June, and hopes to get out around the middle of May

How's Biggie? We hope she didn't get too tired out during our leave. We were both pretty tired out but are feeling much better, again. Well, it seems like news is scarce around here, at the present, so will say 'bye, for now. Write. Be good.

>Love to all from—the Marines,
>Mick

Dearest Folks,

This is a beautiful morning; the sun is shining so brightly. We really welcome the sun, as we had an unusually long spell of cloudy weather. It looked like rain but just never really got around to it.

We finished discharging 14 girls yesterday. We went with the gang the other day when they went down to Pendleton, to have their chest X-Rays, so when the time comes for us to get out, we will have that done. We will be terrifically busy, soon, when all the gals who signed over, until September, will be getting discharged

Camp Pendleton is a Line Co. Marine Base, down near Oceanside, half way between L. A. and San Diego. It is an immense base, but so strewn out, and so desolate looking, after El Toro. We were so glad that we weren't stationed down there. I suppose, tho, we would like it, too, after a while. It always takes a little time to get used to things, it seems. We really didn't need much time, to get to love El Toro!

I must finish this now so that I can get it out in the morning mail.

Love to all,
Irish

Dearest Folks,

We are really going to be very busy this next week discharging girls. Gobs of Miramir girls are coming up and then there is a big bunch going through Separation from our Station, here, so all in all, we will be getting really busy, again.

Much love,
"Irish"

Dearest Folks,

Hope everyone is well at home. Mick and I are both chipper. Hope the weather is good for the crops, etc. We have been having very nice weather, typically California style, cloudy and cool in the mornings, and sunny and nice after about 10 a.m. The evenings are always plenty cool, it seems. The mountains around our Station are beautiful at this time of year. I think I will never get tired of looking at the mountains. Wish that Minnesota had some to look at. Ha.

We are planning on going to L. A. and Hollywood this week-end. We figure we better take advantage of these week-ends because we don't know how many more we will have.

The Captain put our letters through asking for our transfer to Washington, but of course from here, it goes to the Commanding General of Marine Air West Coast, at Miramar, (near San Diego), and then from him it goes to the Commandant of the Marine Corps, at Headquarters, Washington, D. C., for approval. In the meantime, we will interview all the rest of the girls here at El Toro, so we will be ready, for transfer, about the 15th of July, if we get approved. We will be letting you know, one way, or the other, as soon as we know, for sure.

All take care of yourselves.

Love to each,
"Irish"

Dearest Folks,

Everyone is thinking mostly in terms of our Farewell party now, more or less. I don't know if Mick wrote you about it, in full particulars yet, or not. Of course, it is rather hard to tell anything for certain, as they are constantly changing the plans, it seems, trying to improve upon them. It is to be in Tom Breneman's, in Hollywood, and I don't know whether, or not, it will be broadcast, but you might be listening in. It is to be the night of August 14th, and the dinner is to start at approximately 8:30 (Pacific Time.) They are really planning a gala affair.

We discharged 13 girls yesterday. The big bunch of those left here will be discharged, on the 20th, and the last of us enlisted girls will be discharged on the 26dth—so they say now, at least. So, at best, it certainly won't be long now.

Mick is over helping in the Education Office this morning. She has helped over there once before and really enjoys it, too.

Mick and I have started our "civilian buying" and believe you me; it certainly seems strange to be in selecting clothes after this period when we didn't have to think about that. Mick and I did a big washing last night, including our "whites" getting them ready for the big party, in Hollywood, next week. We wore them, on

Catalina, and really slayed the natives. So many people remark about how pretty they are. WE LOVE THEM!

Until tomorrow,
Much love to all,
"Irish"

Dearest Folks,

I guess we didn't tell you about our experience Sunday. We went out to the Naval Dry Docks, again, and went all through the "Boise", a light cruiser, and the "Admiralty Island", one of our baby-flattops. We had seen in the Los Angeles paper that our battle-wagon, the "Maryland "was in the harbor, but when we got there they informed us that the Maryland had only been in three days and had set sail again, so we missed seeing that one. Of course we had been on another baby flattop but never before had we been on a light cruiser.

It was a new and very interesting experience. We saw the catapult and the place where they carry two of our new scout-observation planes, the "Seahawk." We also saw the main batter of 6" rifles and the secondary battery. The men aboard the "Boise" were very proud because they had carried Douglas Mac Arthur on two different occasions, and the Boise had been his flagship during the siege of Borneo. We're going to keep watching in the papers and as soon as some of our battleships come in, we're going to try to get on them. We just love that.

This coming Monday—being Labor Day—we have off. That will make a nice, long weekend, from Saturday noon to Tuesday morning. We plan on going to stay in the Service Girl's Dormitory, in Hollywood and take in a lot of free broadcasts, maybe go out to the Hollywood Bowl some evening, etc.

Love to each,
Mick

Dearest Folks,

We went over to UCLA the other day to see about admission. Of course the fall semester is about to begin shortly, and they have been filled with students months ago. We got application blanks and will have to submit a transcript of our High School and College credits to their Board of Admissions, in November. We also plan to try the U. of Minnesota., and perhaps several other colleges, if we finally settle on going back to college. Quite a bit will depend on this job Mick wrote you about.

> More later,
> "Irish"

Santa Ana, California

Dear Folks,

Just a few lines tonight to tell you we were discharged, today, about 10 o'clock. It was really a bunch of sad girls, I'm telling you. Being a Marine was a most wonderful experience and we have that to be thankful for.

The barracks tonight are just like a morgue—so quiet. It's unbelievable in so short awhile—it was such a busy, busy, place. We are staying here, at the Barracks, tonight, and will go over to Mayme's tomorrow night. We are going to rest for several days before we look around at the employment situation.

If we find something we like, no doubt we'll stay for awhile, at least. It would be awfully hard to leave with a winter coming on, so shortly, in Minnesota. Well, don't put too much stock in this yet, as it is all very indefinite.

> More later and love,
> Mick

Dear Folks,

Hope that everyone and everything at Home is 4.0. We are fine, but rather tired, today.

Yesterday morning we dolled all up in our "whites" and, if I do say so myself, they really "looked sharp," and we proceeded to go to Long Beach and the Naval Dry Docks to see the two ships that were on display for the public. The AH Hospital ship, the U.S.S. Comfort and the destroyer the U.S.S. Zellars. We had been reading about them in the paper and were very interested to see them. We were very lucky to get a ride from right outside our barracks, with a fellow from the Station, directly into Long Beach.

He told us that he makes that run every Sunday morning taking film back to the Navy Station at San Pedro and usually someone else rides with him, sort of a steady customer. He told us, however, to call im at the theater anytime that we wanted to go, and he would be glad to take us, if he had room. He was very nice.

There is only one bus on Sunday morning and that is at 9:03 and that would get us into Long Beach much later. We rode with him to within a couple blocks of St. Anthony's church and were in amply time for the 9 o'clock mass.

We went to Holy Communion and then they invited us along with a gob of other service people to have breakfast with them in the basement of the Catholic school. We went just for the fun of it. It happened to be the graduation of all the St. Anthony High school kids and we saw all of them marching out of church in their caps and gowns.

We then went downtown and looked around and then went to the Hilton Hotel to sit in their lobby and rest a bit before we went out to the drydocks. We met a lot of people while there, including a cute Army Lt. from Sioux City just back from the European theater, and a Navy chief from off this destroyer, the Zellars, and several other Navy Lieutenants. We really had a lot of fun, and everyone of them remarked and remarked about our darling white uniforms. They just couldn't get over how nice they were, and all of them said, as we have heard so many times before, that they are the nicest of any of the Women in Service uniforms. Of course we heartily agree, as you know. Ha.

Talk about a mob of people out at the Drydocks. They estimated there were about ½ million people. You never saw such a crowd. We took one look at that line of people and said to ourselves that, even though it wasn't the polite thing to do, we went to the head of the line and, after a little Irish "line, the S.P's said we didn't have to stand in that line that we should go right ahead and go aboard. We walked up the gangplank in style.

Most of the civilians just got to see a certain portion of the damaged ship. It was the first time a damaged ship was ever open to the public.

When we looked around a wee bit, one of the Officers, who had been aboard when the Japanese kamikaze plane struck, came and offered to show us all around the ship. Of course we accepted his invitation.

It was very, very interesting. Honestly sometimes I think we will go "overboard" over ships and planes, we love them so much. The plane made a direct hit on one of the wards that was full of causalities, from the war, and right into the operating rooms where the Drs. And Nurses were just ready to perform a couple of operations. There were 31 killed outright, and more that 50 injured. It certainly was terrible.

You see the hospital ships don't have any armament to protect themselves, according to the Geneva Convention so no nation is supposed to fire on any Hospital ship. It is clearly marked with big red crosses and they are fully illuminated, so there can be no mistaking their identity. The Japs, of course, don't abide by any conference ruling, and more than that, they say they just consider them "Repair Ships" fixing the fellows up so they can go into combat again. They think this makes them free to fire upon. Some way of looking at it, isn't it?

We certainly enjoyed our trip through the ship. Today we have told different ones about our experience and they just about knock themselves out, thinking how we always get around to such interesting things.

Mick taught over on the other side this morning, and we have to go over there tomorrow again to teach "Submarines." They are getting in new Gunners all the time. We have quite a few pilots over on this side now, just coming back from Overseas. I think they will be starting classes shortly. They don't make them attend, right away; they give them a little time to recuperate, so to speak.

Well, I guess this is about all for this time. Oceans of love to all from both of us.

Irish

Dearest Folks at Home,

How's everyone at home this nice, cool morning? Hope you're all well. We're just fine but a little tired after an interesting experience last night. We had to stay on the base this weekend as it was our Duty Section's turn, so last night we got a ride into Hollywood and went to the NBC studio and saw the "Parade of Stars." Perhaps you heard it over the radio. It was on for two complete hours from 7 to 9. We sat right down in the second row from the stage and they paraded and performed right in front of us.

I'll list the ones we saw and heard in person. Bob Burns, Cass Daley, Abbott and Costello, Dinah Shore, Gracie Allen, Jack Haley and Pernny, George Burns, Rudy Vallee, Billie Burke, Xavier Cugat, Great Gildersleeve (Harold Perry), Ed

Gardner as Archie from "Duffie's Tavern,") Art Linkletter, Wm. Bendix, Don Wilson and Jack Benny. Ralph Edwards who is the star of "Truth or Consequences", Betty Rose and Parkycarkus, Bob Hope and Jerry Colonna. Wasn't that a bunch to see all at once? We were really tickled to have the opportunity to see all of them, so close and "for free." What an experience.

No word from Washington, as yet. Just wait until we are all united again and we'll be living out here in California. We'll take you to all the nice places to eat out here, Knott's Berry Farm, and all the others. We'll really celebrate, won't we?

This is all the "scuttlebutt" that I have for today, so will close for now—until tomorrow.

Much love to all from both of us.
Mickey.

These are but a "sampling" of excerpts, from letters written Home. I hope you enjoyed the insight provided into the War years of late 1943-late 1946.

I would like to close this section of my book with a poem I found. The Author is unknown.

> The old rocking chair is vacant today,
>   For Grandma's no longer in it.
> She's off in the car, to the office or shop,
>   Just buzzing around every minute.
> No one puts her back on the shelf;
>   She's versatile, forceful, dynamic.
> That isn't a pie in the oven you smell,
>   Her baking today, is ceramic.
> She doesn't believe in early to bed,
>   Or seeking a warm comfy nook.
> Her typewriter clackety-clacks, all through the night,
>   For Grandma;s writing a book.
> She never takes a look at her yarn,
>   It would slow her steady advancing,
> She won't tend the babies for you anymore,
>   For Grandma's taking up dancing.
> She isn't content with the crumbs of old age,
>   Or meager, second-hand knowledge.
> Don't bring out mending for Grandma to do,
>   For Grandma's gone back to college!!

BIBLIOGRAPHY

Any given facts, or figures, regarding numbers, or precise details, regarding planes, ships, or any other material, has been taken from one of the three books listed below. They deserve the full credit.

WORLD WAR II, Mc COMBS, DONALD and FRED L. WORTH, 1983

HISTORY of MARINE CORPS AVIATION IN WORLD WAR II, SHERROD, ROBERT, 1952

AMERICAN WOMEN and WORLD WAR II, WEATHERFORD, DORIS, 1990

978-0-595-83726-7
0-595-83726-3

Printed in the United States
53366LVS00004B/52-156